ALEXANDER MASTERS

# A Life Discarded

### 148 Diaries
### Found in a Skip

4th ESTATE · London

4th Estate
An imprint of HarperCollins*Publishers*
1 London Bridge Street
London SE1 9GF
www.4thEstate.co.uk

First published in Great Britain in 2016 by 4th Estate
This 4th Estate paperback edition published in 2017

1

A catalogue record for this book
is available from the British Library

ISBN 978-0-00-813081-7

Typeset in Postscript Minion and Photina
Printed and bound in Great Britain by Clays Ltd, St Ives plc

**MIX**
Paper from
responsible sources
FSC™ C007454

For Dido Davies,
who was blissful.
1953–2013

A nice day in general; just enjoying myself.
No particular thoughts, except perhaps
I'd like to change my life.

# PART ONE

## Mystery

# 1 2001: The Skip

One breezy afternoon, my friend Richard Grove was mooching around Cambridge with his shirt hanging out, when he came across this skip:

Only partially filled, it was resting in an old yew hedge, on a stub of dead-end road. Richard squeezed between the scuffed yellow metal and the hedge and wandered through what had once been an old orchard. Tree stumps, sliced off at ankle height, glistened smoothly in the sun. Pear and apple branches were piled up beside a wood-chewer, waiting to be turned into chips. Beyond this cleared woodland, spreading like a pool of bleach among the grass and flowers, was a building site. A large Arts and Crafts house was being modified. The roof had gone. Underneath, two storeys of red brick walls were cordoned off by corrugated metal fencing. It seemed the property was being exposed to the wind for a good rinse-out. A lot of ancient professors live in this part of Cambridge, dozing on their laurels, shuffling about in worn-out cars. They give the place a musty feel; it needs the occasional airing.

Although Richard had lived nearby for most of his life, this house was so well hidden behind hedges and trees that he hadn't known it existed. By pressing his eye against a gap between the metal fencing posts, he could see the remains of a porch. The wooden column holding up the roof had been snapped, like a knee.

Richard returned to the skip, peered in and became suddenly agitated. Something inside had caught his attention. He stood on tiptoe in an attempt to put his arms over the top and reach down, but his arms weren't long enough. With his shoulders still hunched over the metal, he slid along the skip until he reached the low end and, after looking around unsuccessfully for something to stand on, tried to tip himself over the edge and slide in – but he wouldn't tip. Professor Richard Grove is an energetic man, a world expert on the ecology of islands, and always eager to get himself dirty; but he's a little plump. Defeated by the skip, he ran off. Half an hour later he reappeared with Dr Dido Davies who is thinner.

Dido clambered in easily (by the tipping method) and slid down the metal slope until her feet rested on a large box. A plastic bath panel split and gave way. Dido dropped half an inch. Something collapsed with a metallic sigh. Dido fell to her hands. Dido – a historian, an award-winning biographer, author of two sex manuals under the pseudonym 'Rachel Swift' and the only person in the world who knows where the bones of Sir Thomas More are buried – could see exactly what had made Richard so excited.

Clustered inside a broken shower basin, wedged into the gaps around a wrenched-off door, flapping in the breeze on top of the broken bricks and slates, were armfuls of books. They had been scattered across the rubble exultantly and anyhow. 'They couldn't have been there more than an hour or two, they looked so fresh,' remembered Dido years later. 'It felt as though the person who had thrown them might be still in the garden, but Richard and I looked – nobody was there. I thought, has someone thrown them away because they've gone loony? Has someone come along after the owner has died and tossed the books out in a fit of rage?'

The discovery reminded her of a story about the Cambridge literary critic Frank Kermode. 'Kermode was moving house, and he had this incredibly important library, all first editions, all signed to him by the authors, all boxed up. But somehow he accidentally gave the boxes to the dustbin men instead of the removal men, and this very personal collection was carted off. He never saw the books again. It was the same with these books in the skip: a feeling of wronged privacy. It was so obvious that they shouldn't be destroyed. You wanted to pick them up. It was nothing to do with keeping them. Just to save them, because whoever had thrown them in the skip had run off only a few minutes ago. These books were alive.'

A few of the volumes had royal emblems embossed on the front:

Others were cheap

exercise pads in stale grey-blue. Many were plain, good-quality hardbacks in old-fashioned, accountancy-office red, stamped with gold letters: 'Heffers, Cambridge'. Others were thin and black, with illustrated boards that might have been based on neurological patterns, and therefore belonged in a medical lab. There were jotters of the sort 1950s policemen brought out of their breast pockets, and small, plump ledgers that I last remember seeing in my school uniform shop in the 1970s. Some of the books had been partially destroyed by water that had long since dried out. The corners of the paper stuck in blocks; stains of rotting metal seeped into the pages from the staples. A box, big enough to contain a head, had landed further into the skip and split with the impact. Inside were more volumes, with covers ranging from post-war sugar card to glistening, oily hardbacks that looked as though they'd been bought that morning. The box had jaunty green print on the sides: 'Ribena! 5d off!'

A chalky notebook that Dido picked up broke like chocolate. Inside, the rotted pages were filled with handwriting, right up to the edges, as though the words had been poured in as a fluid.

It was a diary.

All the 148 books in the skip were diaries.

## 2 The Ribena box

boy or girl

Aged twelve

A person can write five million words about itself, and forget to tell you its name.

Or its sex.

People don't include obvious identifiers in diaries: things such as what they're called or where their home is. They are simply 'I', who lives.

And then dies, and gets dumped in a skip.

It was evident that the author had died. People might burn their intimate diaries before they die, but they don't throw them out where any stranger can pick them up.

Two terrible things happened after the discovery of the diaries.

Richard was being driven home from a party, in Australia, when the driver fell asleep and crashed the car into a tree. One of the most courageous and inventive academics of his generation, he is still alive, jolting in a wheelchair, and being moved around the nursing homes of England.

Several years later, Dido, my writing collaborator for a quarter of a century, was diagnosed with a ten-centimetre neuroendocrine tumour on her pancreas. I went with her to hear the diagnosis. There aren't that many times I've seen real courage – the sort that makes you start with admiration each time you remember it. Top of my list for biblical chutzpah is Dido's bemused calm as we came out of the GP's surgery. 'Well, I've had a nice life,' she said. 'Now, shall we go through these pages of yours in Waitrose's café? It's cooler there.'

A few weeks later she began to clear out her house. She had not progressed far with discovering who owned the diaries. As well as no name or return address, on the pages inside there were no obvious descriptions of the writer's appearance, his or her job, or identifiable details of friends or family members. Everything that a person uses to clarify themselves to another person was missing. Why should 'I' bother to put them there? 'I' knew them already.

What could Dido do with this journal? She couldn't take it to the police – they'd laugh at her. She couldn't burn it – that would be criminal.

She gave them to me. It was now my job: I was to find out who was the rightful heir of these 'living books', and return them.

She'd put the diaries in three boxes. The original Ribena bottle crate had no lid; one side was caved in and the top half-shut-up, like a punched eye. The last person to touch this box before Dido was the person who'd thrown it out. There was nothing written on the outside except those shouts about '5d!' No packaging label. Nothing with an alternative address. One of the hand holes was ripped clean in half.

The biggest box was thin, plain and approximately the length of a thigh. It bulged meatily. Through the gaps in the cardboard I could see strips of lurid-coloured modern journals.

The third container was torso-sized and originally for a Canon portable photocopier ('ZERO warm up time'). It was shiny and strapped down with duct tape. On one edge there was a label, addressed to The Librarian, Trinity College, Cambridge.

Perhaps the diaries belonged to a Trinity don, I thought, and got depressed.

The Ribena box was the one that interested me most.

I imagined the hands of the person who'd pitched it into the skip were still half there, glowing on the cardboard, and wondered if careful scientific analysis could reveal whether the injuries the box had sustained as it landed in the skip were because it had been hurled (perpetrator enraged) or lobbed gently (perpetrator calculating). Using the torch on my mobile phone I peeped through the torn hand hole. The diaries inside had been packed with incompetence. Large dark-coloured journals were separated by single pocket books, leaving narrow shelf-shaped gaps in the layers, like rock caverns. In one corner, a thin hardback had been flattened down with such force that its spine had broken. Many of the books were rotting along the edges, and mossy-coloured, as if I had caught them secretly returning to trees. The cover of one was coated with regular stripes of white mould, like the fungus you get on old cheddar cheese.

I pressed my nose against the hand hole. It smelled crisp and mournful.

There were twenty-seven diaries in this box in total. The first I picked out was a pocketbook: quarter-bound, blue, with a red spine. Inside, a printer's advertisement read 'Denbigh Commercial Books' in a border made of moustache shapes, which made me think of signs swinging in a mid-western breeze and Clint Eastwood clinking into town. On the facing page, the seller had stamped his details in purple ink: 'W. Cannings Ltd,

23/5 Peckham High Street, London'. The price was marked in
the top left-hand corner, handwritten in pencil: 3/10.

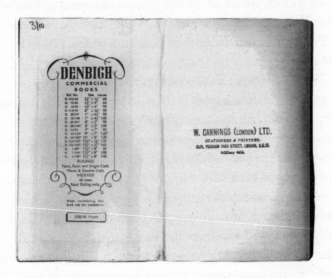

Inside, the pages were crammed to the brim with handwriting. The letters were confident and generous, occupied all
the available space on a page with six words to a line, and apart
from occasional merriments in the letters 'J', 'H' and 'd',

the script continued with almost mechanical regularity from
the front cover to the back. It was not a purpose-made journal.
No printed diary could have been manufactured to
accommodate this writer's need. Some entries were four
thousand words long; a few were even longer; no day was left
alone. It was an ordinary pocket notebook, ambushed by a

person's desperation to record his or her life. At the top of the first page, written inside square brackets, as though it hardly mattered, was the year: 1960.

I felt unexpectedly moved by this detail. A tube I could look down seemed to puncture the blur of the last fifty years and pop out again, fifty miles away in South London, beside the diarist as he (in my mind it was already male: there was a destructive element about the way the writing filled up the page – like a boy stamping on fresh snow) walked up Peckham High Street. I put my eye to this tube and blinked at my new friend. Who was he? Why was he moving at such a pace? Was there something about him that already said, 'You will end up in a skip'? I saw Cannings the stationer's as a low-ceilinged room, the brass bell above the door shaking off the noise of the traffic outside as my man entered. I imagined a flight of steps in the centre of the shop leading to a basement store, and a stout assistant gloomily wrapping up a parcel beside the cash register. I had not read a word of these books, yet already the diarist was clear in my mind: his height, the colour of his fedora hat, his energetic walking pace, the fact that his brown shoes were not brogues (I hate brogues).

The entire Cannings volume covered two months, from October 16th to December 16th, and many pages had excited-looking comments, put in as after-thoughts, running like bubbles up the margins. It was as though the book had been scooped into wordy water and brought out, gurgling.

I noticed that the covers were warped, and thought for a moment that the book had been bent, as if crammed into a pocket that was too small; but then I discovered the distortion was caused by a small mound of folded inserts stuffed at the back of the diary. The writer, unable to stop himself rushing on even when he'd reached the end of the book, had spilled his text onto torn-up segments of letter paper. Scribbled up the margin of one of these extra sheets, in handwriting as pale as a whisper, were the first words I read:

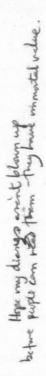

Hope my diaries aren't blown up
before people can read them – they have immortal value.

The Cannings diary feels as though it was produced by someone mesmerised by writing. The letters in the body of the text are large, and have been put down at speed in soft pencil or ballpoint pen.

The next book I picked out was a cheap, thin, black notebook, covered in washable rexine. Here the handwriting was smaller and in blue fountain pen, and from a year later:

> I must continue with this starving life – the long slogging
> hours with only a sandwich for lunch – the work must so
> fill & dominate my soul . . .

He is working on one project in particular – the greatest of his
life. But, as with all the things that matter to him profoundly
(such as his name, his sex, his address, his physical appearance),
he doesn't say what this project is. It is simply 'it'. He doesn't
describe 'it' even vaguely, either because that would be
dangerous, because he is a spy or a bomb maker; or because
'it' is so obvious to him, so much a part of him, that 'it' must
be on a par with his existence.

> I cling to life very desperately – feel I could do great things
> – very afraid of physical disaster, nothing could be worse –
> could not bear to die before I had given of my gifts to the
> community – have already worked & suffered so to bring
> my gifts towards fruition.

In some sections of this journal there are more crossings-
out than others, more words have been underscored and the
handwriting is more uneven: <u>injure</u>, <u>atmosphere</u>, <u>doesn't
believe me</u>!! <u>so hungry</u>! I'll <u>kill</u> them!

> One must live dangerously, take risks, or one otherwise is
> in an ordinary metier all along . . . I now see I can do it.

# 3 The Freshest diaries . . .

I had a dream, of beating Peter up.
**Aged fifty-five**

The freshest diaries contain the oldest handwriting.

These are in the second box – the one the size of a thigh – and are as out of place beside the 1960s diaries I found in the Ribena crate as bubblegum squashed on an Etruscan pot: one is indignant green, similar to fish-and-chip-shop mushy peas; another is milky parma violet; a tangerine version looks as oily and dimpled as the fruit. The diaries in the Ribena box suggest Britain after the war. By contrast, these books in the thigh box couldn't have existed before the 1990s. They've been produced using computer-aided chemical processes. They've made long container journeys from South-East Asia by sea, and they have a texture similar to thin, soft rubber; it's disgusting, like a sheath.

The endpapers cracked when I eased them open.

The writing in the thigh box is also different to that in the earlier books. It's done in blue-black ink with a medium nib, never biro, and makes me think of escaping maggots. The early diaries from the 1960s are written in ebullient letters. Four words are sometimes all it takes to fill the width of a page. In these modern books 'I' crams fourteen words to a line. The height of the letters is the same as the thickness of the pen nib. The shapes of the letters have changed too: 'h's are often written with just a vertical line, or (in small, quick words such as 'that' and 'the') ignored entirely; 'u's and the round bit of 'd's are as flat as pennies. Everything is wriggly or sat on. But after the initial shock this hand is not too difficult to read.

If I was "God", I would
strike the people all dead.

Two lines of text can easily be slid into each gap between the printed rulings:

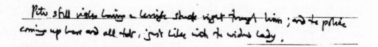

Peter still risks having a knife stuck right through him;
and the police coming up here and all that,
just like with the widow lady.

And, whereas in the early books the diarist wrote always on or parallel to the line, here he runs at precisely two degrees to the horizontal, suggesting that his arm is constrained, as if by a piece of rope:

It was in the news that a man has been let out of prison – was wrongfully imprisoned since 1975, twenty three years; myself been shut up at Peter's for one year more;

It was in the news that a man has been let out of prison –
was wrongfully imprisoned since 1975, twenty three years;
myself been shut up at Peter's for one year more.

Yet these diaries are unquestionably by the same person as the ones in the Ribena box. It's not the handwriting that gives the author away, it's the sense of urgency. In both cases, the text charges in from a previous book in the top-left-hand corner of the first possible page and, two hundred sheets later, in the last millimetres of the closing blank side, explodes off towards tomorrow. Removal men couldn't squeeze in more. The lurid-coloured modern volumes each contain 150,000 words and cover roughly two months of entries, or 2,500 words a day. The typical English human can write thirty words per minute. Assuming no pauses for thought or to relax hand muscles, this man is therefore spending an average of an hour and twenty-three minutes each day offloading his thoughts onto paper. It is never less than forty minutes. On rare occasions it is as much as three hours.

There are no crossings-out or hesitations. Once or twice the ink fades abruptly in the middle of a word, in the space of a few letters. But the writer must have spare cartridges close by, because instantly it spurts away again, hauling the day on.

Life is an emptiness in these late books. All talk about the Great Project is gone. There is no mention of 'it'. He sees nobody and goes nowhere. 'I' describes himself as 'ruined', lost', 'sacrificed'. There has been a smash of all his hopes. It is not only the man called Peter who is responsible for this catastrophe; 'I' several times accuses 'those who are stuffed with sleep'.

The writer refers to this man called Peter as his 'gaoler' – a 'cruel' person.

*I just wish I could put my hands round his throat and strangle him – throttle him to death.*

I just wish I could put my hands round his throat
and <u>strangle</u> him – throttle him to death.

We never see Peter. The writer never describes him physically. We smell him. 'Pongy Peter', 'I' labels him; 'Stinky Peter'. Occasionally, particularly at night, we hear him. His footsteps creak along the corridor below; there is a rattle at the rear of the house and a rush of water: he has gone to the toilet.

*It is still a riddle to me, how all the stink of his wicklery comes up to the back landing when he has a crap – if it comes up through the drainpipes or the ventilators or what. Or if the smell seeps out of his bedroom from the pipe to his washbasin*

It is still a riddle to me, how all the stink of his wickery [going to the
toilet] comes up to the back landing when he has a crap – if it comes
up through the drainpipes or the ventilators or what. Or if the smell
seeps out of his bedroom from the pipe to his washbasin.

18

Occasionally, Peter creeps into 'I's room. What happens next is hardly believable. He steals 'I's belongings! Books, valuable letters, volumes of the diaries themselves. He sets light to his haul in the garden.

*I think Peter must have burnt all E's photos, and a lot of the music – took advantage when I was in hospital.*

I think Peter <u>must</u> have burnt all E's photos, and a lot of the music – took advantage when I was in hospital.

What is going on? Why doesn't the diarist stop this hateful behaviour?

Peter is a detestable man.

*He seems indestructible, like Nelson Mandela.*

He seems indestructible, like Nelson Mandela.

# 4  Flatface

May just look back on a life of struggle, at
the age of sixty or so – and feel deeply
sad, because in spite of various talents, of
great beauty, have come to nothing.

**Aged twenty-one**

Six of the diaries in the thigh box are 'Max-Val' exercise books,
stapled along the centre-fold, with paper made out of oat
biscuits. The colour of these dreary little volumes is washed-
out, Latin-class blue. Printed on the back of each is a set of
Arithmetical Tables giving the lengths for cloth measure
(2½ inches = 1 nail), the amount of grass needed to make up a
'Truss' (56lbs of Old Hay; 60lbs, New Hay; 36lbs of Straw),
and, my favourite, 'Apothecaries' Weight for mixing medicines':
20 grains = 1 Scruple.

Inside the books is a rapidly hand-drawn cartoon strip in
blue ink. There are between two and eight frames per page.
Nowadays it would be called a graphic novel. The scenes are of
different sizes and always boxed in. The figures in the story are
dressed in cloaks and repeatedly caught in moments of
persecution or shock. The faces are distorted. But what's going
on is anybody's guess.

The narrative does not progress obviously; it is like a set of
flash photographs taken of a troupe of melodramatic puppets.
The only constant figure is an androgynous and rhinoceros-
nosed face:

This face is always viewed from the left, angled down, just off the silhouette. It appears in each frame of the cartoon – a total of well over two thousand times – and always produced in the same way, with nine fundamental lines: one for the forehead, two for the big nose, another to make the priggish upper lip, the chin and jaw are produced by a single wiggle that looks vaguely Arabic, a down stroke for a dimple and three quick movements to make up the eye. Hair (sometimes slicked, sometimes dishevelled) is a rush of slashes or curls on top. Most of the time this wig-wearing flatfish of a face doesn't reflect much. It appears to be a force of creamy benignity. At its most irritating it represents poetic suffering. Sometimes it has a body coming off it, sometimes not. It is repeated so often that you begin to feel ill at the sight of the thing.

The flatface's name is (usually) Clarence. It can also be called Rhubarb or Porbarb or John.

Sometimes he's in prison:

with his two cellmates, the 'Keeper', who has a jaw like a
casserole pot . . .

. . . and a rubber-faced monstrosity called Worful:

'Clarence' Flatface lives in the past. Sometimes he's out of clink and down the tavern, being asked difficult maths questions . . .

*"What's two and two?"*

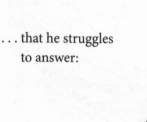 ... that he struggles
to answer:

At other times, as 'John', Flatface is living at the time the
cartoon is being drawn, in the early 1960s. In these
contemporary frames 'John' might be lying in a fancy
deckchair, with a Martini:

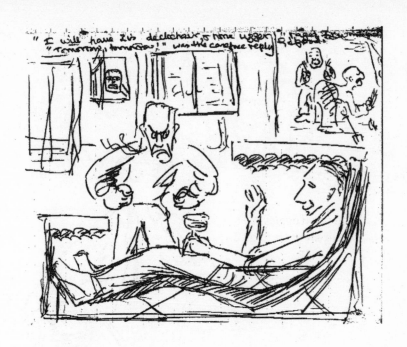

*"I will have zis deckchair, & none uzzer" raged Irwin.*
*"Tomorrow, tomorrow!" was the carefree reply.*

How did he get into this chair? Why is Irwin (who turns out to be Flatface's brother) speaking in a German accent? What are those two people up in the air doing – planting carrots? Since when did deckchairs have foot canopies?

Once, as 'Clarence', Flatface becomes a king . . .

. . . which makes him grumpy.

Another time, Flatface's days appear to be numbered:

This story never settles down – except for Flatface's eternal presence. Every fifteen or twenty pages the strip is abruptly cut off and a whole side is given over to this disturbing profile:

Relieved, the writer then picks up the story again and presses on.

This isn't a cartoon strip, it's a set of narrative false starts 'tethered by a face. But whose face? Not 'I's own, surely. A person this self-obsessed would want to explore his features, not freeze them. This face is a symbol for someone or something. Give it a few more years and it will evolve into a pictogram and join the Chinese alphabet.

There is only one occasion on which 'I' does not limit himself to the nine essential lines and allows Clarence to look at the reader full on. To emphasise the horror of the revelation, it is also the only time 'I' uses colour:

# 5 The Torso box

Got two obsessions – that I'm going to be an author;
and that I'm going to choke.

**Aged twenty-one**

In 2005, I left Cambridge and rented a shooting lodge in Suffolk, and the diaries became a makeshift boot stand. In 2006, my girlfriend Flora and I went to London to house-sit for a pianist. The torso-sized printer box became a cocktail table; the box the size of a thigh propped up a chair; the Ribena crate, too wonky to be of any use, got kicked under the Steinway.

In 2007, Dido was told she had neuroendocrine cancer of the pancreas. In 2009, that it had spread.

I had known Dido for twenty-five years. When I first met her my father was dying – she saw me through that; I was twenty-one and idiotic. She was twelve years older. She grew me up, taught me how to think, how to write, how to be.

Pancreatic neuroendocrine cancer is the same disease that killed Steve Jobs, and is why he was able to develop the iPad and the iPhone. If he'd had ordinary pancreatic cancer (as almost all newspapers insisted on giving him at the time) he'd have been dead before the MacBook. Neuroendocrine tumours can be very slow-growing. Some people live the rest of their natural life with them, as long as they do not spread.

Dido's tumour had seeded over her liver. Its spores had crowded into her blood.

The consultant at Dido's local hospital was contemptible: bullying and scary. I arranged for Dido's case to be moved to the Royal Free in London, a European Centre of Excellence for neuroendocrine cancer. There was a scan due in six weeks' time; I had to be on the phone every morning to reduce that to ten days. The NHS is a wonderful organisation as long as you learn how to kick it. There were anti-cancer diets to be researched, exercise programmes to be uncovered, high-absorption liposomal curcumin to be ordered in from California at $95 a 100ml bottle (produced by a man who, I subsequently discovered, was being pursued on a manslaughter charge), electrically-operated pomegranate squeezers to be shipped from Istanbul, a remarkable peer-reviewed but forgotten therapeutic from Sweden to be investigated. In fact, why are we still talking? I had to get on . . .

During the five years Flora and I stayed in the London house, I'd occasionally catch sight of the boxes and remember their contents with dislike: that terrible face; those tiny scuttling letters; 'I's sense of destiny and devotion to an unknown, perhaps unknowable project of vital human importance followed by the catastrophic failure of all his plans. Despite the glistening orange and shocking pea-green covers of some of the books, I thought of them as pallid objects. I had the same feeling towards the diaries in these boxes as I do towards the ghosts in an M.R. James story: thrilling, but forces of absence; not so much evil as empty of good. They marked a time when Dido was well. They emphasised that she might be dying. They were hateful.

Occasionally, I'd creep under the Steinway and peer inside the Ribena crate. But I didn't study the books. I reversed back out between the legs of the piano with the slightly appalled sensation that I was escaping quicksand.

Flora and I moved again in 2011, to Great Snoring in Norfolk, by which time I had forgotten about the diaries. They were just three more boxes among the thousand or so that I drag about like Marley's chain every time I change landlords. I shoved them into the back of the van with the rest, yanked them out among the chickens and runner ducks at the other end and dropped them into a storeroom.

At which point the Ribena box burst open and twenty-seven diaries spilled out.

One of them featured a bloodbath.

The Collins 'Three Day Royal Diary' is greeny-blue, not much bigger than a jacket potato and caved in halfway up the spine, as if it has been crushed by a spasmodic grip. I tested it, waving it around the chicken yard in Great Snoring with various holds of my own. Only a left hand could make this type of depression. It was a gesture I imagined an outdoor preacher would use as he clutched the Gospels and harangued cowboys.

An inside page printed with useful information calls New Year's Day 'the Circumcision'.

Once again, the diarist's handwriting races into the book many sides before the official diary section starts:

> November 19th, Saturday
> Spent most of today painting. Perhaps it is the best I've ever done, more like <u>Van Gogh</u> than anything else.

and 126 pages and four weeks later shoots out from the bottom of the last possible page, with the words 'watched her go with foreboding . . .'

In between, 'I' describes a stabbing.

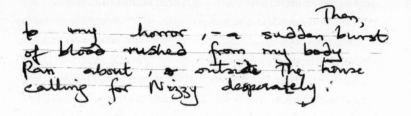

Then,
to my horror, – a sudden burst
of blood rushed from my body
Ran about, & outside the house
calling for Nizzy desperately.

never lost so much [blood] so suddenly before
in my life,

felt terribly afraid.

Who has stabbed him? Why? Who is Nizzy? 'I' doesn't say.
Where is he outside? Bleeding on the road? In the garden?
I picture him leaping about a rockery as he clutches at his
wound. What time is it? It might be first thing in the morning,

because 'I' reports that he's in his pyjamas. But then he's a painter, so it could be any time of day.

Nothing about the methodical, evenly-spaced way 'I' forms his letters changes during this dramatic episode. If anything, a calm comes over the text. 'I' calculates that he will need a 'blood transfusion' and thoughtfully returns to the house to call his doctor so the hospital will be prepared for his arrival and have the machinery set up. But the sheet of telephone numbers beside the phone is missing – an absence that's as good as finding the telephone wires have been cut. Weeping 'with the added frustration', 'I' scrabbles around for the phone list.

Then, abruptly, the squall ends.

The bleeding stops. Nizzy comes home and turns out to be his mother. 'Crying in that uncontrollable way I sometimes have', he tells her about the blood. Nizzy says he 'is fussing unnecessarily'.

Our mystery diarist hasn't been stabbed, slashed his wrists or fallen out of a window into a greenhouse. He's suffering 'because of my sex'.

The poor man's got the curse.

He's a woman.

# 6    A Chapter of curses

I was born to love and be a woman as well as an artist
Really have a very feminine nature, though not
all lipsticky and screams.

**Aged twenty-one**

What man hasn't wanted to gawp around a woman's thoughts?

It wasn't just gloom and convenience that led me back to these books. It was eroticism. I was desperate to look at them again.

'You want to know what I, a woman, think when I'm pacing around on my own?' the author of the diaries seemed to be saying. 'Settle back. Listen close. The answer takes 148 books.'

If I read these pages I would be like Tiresias, the Greek seer who spent seven years as a woman after being bitten by a snake. Asked by Zeus whether women or men enjoyed sex more, Tiresias replied that women got nine times more pleasure, and was promptly blinded by Hera.

Study these diaries, and I would learn secrets for which it was worth being blinded.

I pulled the curtains in my study in Great Snoring, shut the door and locked myself in. Where would 'I' take me first? The bedroom?

To my shock she took me to the toilet.

'I's curse began when she was fourteen, took over her life when she was twenty, at its worst ruined three weeks out of every four (one lost to fear, one to pain, one to exhaustion), and was not considered bad enough to need medical attention.

> Soon the tummy ache came on. It was not as bad as when it gets me extremely, but did feel awful; it certainly the worst pain to endure that I have experienced. Took pills, & knelt on the floor, just living for the pain to go.

I knew I should take all three boxes back to Cambridge police station and, if they remained unclaimed, after a suitable time have them incinerated. I was a pervert to do anything else. I was not a decent human being. The world has no business to gawp at a woman at a moment like this. The writer was already describing things in a way that makes it clear she never expects or wants anyone else to hear about them, let alone put them in a biography.

Thrilled, I lit a fire, backed myself onto an armchair and kept reading. I could hardly believe my luck.

In the early books, 'I' talks about her period in the same way that addicts at the homeless hostel where I once worked talked about a hit of heroin. It makes her feel blissful, as you do on a Sunday morning when you open your eyes, see the day has started long ago and slip back into dreams knowing there's not the slightest need to get up.

> Felt very warm & sleepy – a sort of healthy sleepiness of period. In morning, felt everything very beautiful, & that I'm beautiful myself. Men seem swerb [delightful].

She likes to see men weeping in the week before her curse. She pictures them sinking to their knees with griefs that are difficult to soothe. Once, on the bus to her sixth-form college during this pre-curse week, she was distracted by a juicy reverie. She imagined an opera in which a young girl 'is kept under the domination of her possessive jealous guardian, who has arranged for her to marry a man who is young & handsome but whom she does not love'.

All the while she was on the bus, the hormonal diarist hungered over this promising situation. She imagined that perhaps the young girl's guardian employs a painter to do her portrait, and forbids the painter to touch or talk to her. 'But the enthusiastic painter cannot work in silence for long . . . '

Hearing the guardian's footsteps they spring back to their proper positions. [The painter] stalks off, dripping brushes as he goes.

Yet when 'I' finally lets us see what this seducing artist who is about to make off with the girl looks like, it is a startling surprise. Sprawled amid the cascades of brocaded silks and velvet, he squats like a braised toad: 'middle-aged, rather ugly, a red-head & a Bohemian, perhaps a little plump'.

The next morning, the diarist's bleeding began.

Feeling generally washed out from period. Heard some Beethoven on wireless as I looked out of kitchen window onto the daffodils and garden beauty – and felt a deep & poignant sorrow which can only be felt by a rather heavy loss of blood. Such a profound effect have bodily states on one – so that I am cheerful even though I have no post or prospects, & utterly depressed.

In 1960, the monthly pattern of her period changed. It lost its euphoric element; the entire process became hateful. The pre-menstrual tension of her impending curse hung against her groin, pressed at her bladder, grew around her stomach – waiting to burst. A 'congestion of body and soul!'

Her male GP says none of this is worrying – this was just what it was to be a woman. She has, he murmurs revoltingly, 'ripened'.

The whole human race drives me to a frenzy of irritation, my habitual courtesy a very thin shell over my real passions.

And then the 'congestion' broke, sometimes to 'within half an hour of its due time'; other times it's days late or early. Once, her period started in the middle of a Mozart sonata she was playing on her employer's grand piano. Another time, she was on the bus again, watching her reflection in the window and imagining she was in Versailles. Suddenly, she was on the Niagara Falls.

> Felt I could hardly bear it today, when the flow came on again. It isn't necessarily even pain, but a sort of queasiness, or faintness in the tummy or upheaval in the whole body. Don't think I could keep any post with it like this, it is so incapacitating, but what can one do about it? Have lost a week over it as to doing anything – no work, nothing . . .

If an exam falls on one of these days, tough. If 'I' needs to do something that requires close attention, fine mechanical behaviour or being more than five minutes from the nearest lavatory, hard cheese. It's a wonder girls get up at all, let alone go to school and beat the socks off the boys at exams.

Between the ages of twenty and twenty-five, as soon as the diarist tries to get started on anything, Nature sticks out a toe, trips her over and spends the next four or five days punching her in the stomach:

> How ill it makes you feel; one can do nothing but hug one's pain.

beating her on the head:

felt dreadfully giddy, felt I couldn't even focus straight.

poking her ears:

> Went down slowly to the Post Office. Was afflicted with
> hyperaesthesia, could hardly bear the noise of passing
> cars, couldn't bear sound today.

yanking out her innards:

> the pain & disturbance of a plunging womb.

and stopping her heart:

> Rose in morning, but soon had that overwhelming
> tummyache and consequent faintness. The pain was awful
> – lay sprawled on my untidy bed, fainting, and sweating
> all over, my blouse undone. After about an hour or so, the
> tablets took effect and the pain went; felt cold after that,
> put back on my jersey, got a hot water bottle. When that
> awful hour was over, lay back in bed, became very sleepy,
> and with an unusually low pulse.

In October, she starts to develop 'ugly feelings' at her sixth-
form college:

> Feel curiously criminal desires, not so far from
> committing them – would like to attack someone,
> threaten them, hit them, even knife them; burn the
> coats in the cloakroom; break things.

She loses jobs, friends, including two possible boyfriends;

the curse buggers up her holidays, her sleep, her eating – but, astonishingly, she never loses her self-control. She still walks down the street with a calm expression, as though nothing were wrong. 'Don't show it, because it isn't right.' She is a person of great fortitude.

Think I am rather superstitious over the period, because it is exclusively a female process, & mysterious, not like a cold in the head. Certainly, with the period, have felt iller than anything else had made me feel, worse than measles. Suppose the pain is the burden of womankind; yet it shouldn't by rights be painful, it is a natural process. I imagine people who live nearer the earth don't get it so much, people like peasants & savages.

During her lifetime, 'I' will have had around 450 curses, losing up to thirty-six litres of fluid and membrane, which is equivalent to pouring away her entire blood content six times over.

I tested it at the petrol station the other day: with the nozzle full on, my hand squeezing the lever tight against the grip, it takes one minute and twelve seconds to pump thirty-six litres into my Honda Civic. It's enough petrol to blow up the entire forecourt.

Think the whole business of bladder and bowels is disgusting, and that Nature has shown shocking bad taste in creating such functions.

# 7  Wor

**Aged eighteen(?)**

After an afternoon of studying the diarist, I put all the volumes back in their boxes exactly as I had found them: the old Cannings diary with its great project – the 'it' that <u>MUST BE DONE!!</u> – into the Ribena crate; the lurid modern books with their air of banal murderousness into the thigh box; the seven pads of drawings. I felt it was vital to preserve the order of the books in the boxes – as though even their arrangement captured something living and as yet unknowable about the diarist.

It was as I was about to put the first Max-Val pad of cartoons back into place that I realised who Clarence was. Flicking through the pages one last time, I stopped at a baffling episode in which Flatface (as 'Clarence') is out of prison and walking around a monastic courtyard.

One of the other characters is called Brakenbury. Brakenbury and Clarence? Hang on, isn't that Shakespeare? Malmsey wine? Clarence must be the Duke of Clarence, the butt of Malmsey man. The room Flatface lives in with the Keeper and Worful is therefore the condemned man's cell in the Tower of London. Yes, look! Here it is: *Richard III* . . . Duke of Clarence, *brother to the king*; Sir Robert Brackenbury [spelled with a 'c' in the middle], *Lieutenant of the Tower* . . .

and there, the last name in the list, right at the end of the splendid round-up of extra parts: Bishops, Aldermen, Citizens, Soldiers, Messengers, Murderers, *Keeper* – the boy with a jaw like a casserole pot.

('Wessar' is 'I's word for (I think) 'bottom'.)

Shortly after Brakenbury appears in the cartoon strip, the point is absolutely settled, because in comes Richard himself, looking remarkably like Laurence Olivier:

That's what this is! These strange figures are the actors from the 1955 Olivier film of *Richard III*. The one with the sparse, angular street scenes and Olivier's lizardish king. Clarence is played by John Gielgud.

The reason for the baffling shifts in time in the comic strip is because the modern scenes are showing John Gielgud when he's off set. For example, when he's waiting to go to his brother Irwin's lavatory:

Irwin: *"Damn it all, John, he's gone and pinched "Pride and Prejudice", <u>and</u> he's !!"*
John was more amused than sympathetic.

or being chased by eggs ('I's word for women):

*"I'd love to come out with you Johnnie," said the egg.*

The young diarist is bewitched by John Gielgud. The actor's face does not vary because it is a perfect denotation: those nine lines and the sprouting of hair are her hieroglyph of love.

> Forgot to put in diary, that on Monday night – or rather, Tuesday morning, a swerb dream of Clarence in his brown gown, lying on the ground, weeping, with his head on his sleeve – a vague & c-feel [arousing] & swerb dream. Bother my duties – eugh. Want to have a fling!

Other exercise pads and jotters that I've discovered since contain attempts to start a novel about Gielgud. It's an explosive story. Things constantly happen 'suddenly'. People are repeatedly unexpected. Several times per page a narrative hand pops out and slaps the reader across the face:

John still felt upset, so accordingly partook of a great deal of Dry Martini, more than was perhaps good for him. His sense of injury and self-disgust began to melt away under the soothing effect of the drink and the stimulation of gay companionship. Irwin was also by now very cheerful, becoming more genial and expansive every minute, and waiting continually on Fleurette Blabbage, who proved herself to be extremely fond of shrimp-olive compote and exceptionally fond of mixed cocktail. The egg actually grew quite condescending and gracious after a session of these influences.

"Everyone, listen, Mr Gielgud says he will play to us. Isn't that charming of him?"

John took up a volume of Beethoven's sonatas. The place fell open, as if by itself.

"What a messy page," remarked Fleurette Blabbage.

"That's fingering," Val [John's other brother, both in this story and in real life] informed her. "He's practised this one a lot."

John smiled at them, and put the book up to the rack. His hands stretched hungrily over the keys. Then he began to play.

A simple, delicate, singing melody, touched with magic, passed from the piano to the listening room. Fleurette Blabbage's cynical grin faded. Clunes [Alec Clunes, who played Hastings in the *Richard III* film] leant forward intently. Suddenly Baker listened too. Irwin made a face. And as for John he forgot them all, and his troubles, caught in a spell of sound, in the world of black and white, and undescribed colours, and the infinite. His playing was soft and dreamy; all of a sudden it changed. It grew wild and impassioned. John too. They all started up, with a certain sense of shock. Irwin stopped making faces. After all, John wasn't a bad player – almost good.

Then the first theme returned again. It was like a legend, remote, sounding through distant years. It was magic, mystical. John's playing gave it that quality.

No one paid any attention to Fleurette Blabbage. The egg was gazing at John Gielgud with all her heart. Her large eyes rolled over his face. With them she traced his curling hair, large nose, firm mouth, and stern Gielgud lines.

"Mr Gielgud!" the egg suddenly yelled leaping to her feet. "Stop that at once! What a row! My poor ears! All the notes are wrong!"

'I' is a better artist than a novelist. The drawings can seem clumsy, as though she drew them in a deliberately primitive and rushed style, but they didn't end up in a skip because of her lack of talent. She has an excellent feel for movement and a good sense of weight and balance. There are plenty of professional artists in Cambridge who don't have half her unexpectedness and verve but still make a living with their flaccid still-lives and sculptures with holes in the middle.

The reason for 'I's failure as an artist is in the drawings; but it's not the drawings.

It's the figure of Worful.

Who is Worful?

He doesn't appear in *Richard III*. There's no character in the *dramatis personae* who sounds anything like that, or in Olivier's film. But he's the essential foil in the diarist's strip: the hideous, rubber-faced, cowardly, sycophantic creature who jumps after Flatface across all the pages of the cartoon, belching, vomiting, pulling repulsive faces and betraying everybody.

*But Worful had the necessar torture, after all . . .*

The only time Clarence is laughing rather than looking sanctimonious is when he's enjoying Worful's pain.

The answer comes in the first book of drawings. Written in large letters, in the diarist's youthful hand, it is at the top of the first page before anything else. But this solution is easy to overlook because immediately after writing it 'I' crossed the explanation out, as though the revelation was too painful. It's cost me considerable fussing with the scanner and Photoshop to get rid of the obscuring lines:

Wor is me.

# 8   As soon as I had the idea . . .

> My diary is now a work of art – am not
> afraid of people reading it, though it is so
> intimate.
>
> **Aged twenty-one**

As soon as I had the idea to write a biography of this
anonymous diarist – a biography in which the biographer
doesn't know who his subject is – I was struck by an odd fact.
Whenever I fantasised that she was somebody famous I felt
immediately, and as decisively as if the books had been
dropped on my head, bored.

The great excitement of an anonymous diary is that it might
belong to anybody. Even giving 'I' a name destroyed a vital
thing that made the books interesting – a sense of quiet
universality. I wanted to know what the women I passed in the
street or sat beside on the train were thinking, and these books,
I thought, would tell me. Give the diarist a name and she
became just another stranger who didn't want to accept my
gaze. Imagine that she turned out to be some celebrity and the
books (and my voyeurism) became almost nauseating.

It says a great deal for the diarist that, for the next four years,
she managed to keep me reading without displaying a single
moment of coarseness or impropriety. She has remained,
throughout the guided tour she has given me of her mind,
honest, funny, outlandish . . . and respectable.

When, beyond the grave, I meet this extraordinary ordinary
woman, I will tell her so.

# 9  Nothing is certain

I shall miss me.
**Dido**

Nothing is certain – that's the number-one cancer cliché.
Less than a year after Dido's first course of chemotherapy,
the tumours on her pancreas and liver began to grow again.
On rare occasions, these chemo drugs work. Often they simply
toughen the growths up and make it harder for later therapies
to have an effect.

'We return to the soar and the plunge,' said Dido. 'You're not
going to die, yes you are, no you're not. Whoops, sorry, yes you
are.'

One morning when I went to visit Dido in hospital, the
London consultant, a usually excellent man, had not given her
the correct anti-emetics. Her retching in the hospital toilet
sounded like three men having an argument.

Scientific ignorance, avoidable errors of judgement, the
appalling realisations of hindsight – these are integral to
cancer, not separate from it. They are as much a part of the
disease as the tumours themselves. I do not discuss this
perception with Dido. It is my way of isolating the feeling that
she is easing away and that life has, in some sense I cannot
understand, already allowed death in.

To avoid thinking about dying, we have increased the
amount of work we do on each other's manuscripts – both of
us are writing types of detective story: she, about the hunt for St

Thomas More's bones (she is the only person in the world who knows where they are buried); me, the hunt for 'I'.

In her chapter on More in prison (coincidentally, the same prison where Flatface/Clarence was locked up), Dido had written: *In the Tower kitchens the cook is building a pile of slow-burning hardwood and dry-crackle kindling, with which to stoke his cauldron: More's head, before being stuck on a pole on London Bridge, must be parboiled to the consistency of pasta.*

'What sort of pasta?' I wanted to know. 'Heinz alphabet or *al dente*?'

From my bag, I plucked out a twisting, wriggling object.

'Nooo, I don't think that's a rat,' said Dido, taking it between her pinched fingers. It was a fragment of plastic, milky with age, that I'd found in a mound at the bottom of the Ribena box. 'The second favourite thing for a rat to gnaw is a book spine, and the spines on the diaries are untouched. Their first favourite is an electricity cable.'

A faint, green-tinted segment of the letter 'G' filled up one corner of the piece of plastic.

'But you agree that that's a piece of disintegrated shopping bag?'

'Yes.'

'Then it tells us that our diarist had south-facing windows and is unlikely to be an accountant or a policewoman.'

Dido flicked her infusion tube up and down impatiently, as though it were a cloak hem.

'And here's why,' I continued. 'The reason the books in the Ribena box are packed so badly is because the diarist first put them in this plastic bag, then squashed it into the box. So, if it's not a rat that ruined this bag, it's sunlight, which suggests a south-facing window, that it must have remained in this position for many years, and that the person is not well organised . . .'

Dido dropped the fragment of plastic back into my hand. She had a theory of her own. 'She came from a village or a town.'

'We don't know that. She hasn't said anything about her home yet.'

'We do know it, because she can't find the sheet of telephone numbers when she wants to ring the hospital to arrange a blood transfusion after her curse. Why did she need a sheet of numbers? Why not just ring 999? The reason is, 999 wasn't introduced across the country until the mid-seventies, and she was writing in 1960. 999 was only available in cities then.'

On the train back to Great Snoring I read the rest of the diary from 1960. It is early December. The diarist is 'tired and nervous'. She is in love with several men. One tells her she is 'very sexy'; another is 'a very virile sort' (although 'don't like muscular strength in a man very much, it makes me afraid'), and has the inappropriate name of Mr Weakley.

One evening, 'I' takes herself to see Gilbert and Sullivan's comic opera *Iolanthe*. The fairy Iolanthe has married a human and borne a son who is fairy down to his waist. His legs are human. He is in love with Phyllis, a ward of court, but the Lord Chancellor is in love with her too:

> But there'd be the deuce to pay in the Lords
> If I fell in love with one of my Wards:
> Which rather tries my temper, for
> I'm SUCH a susceptible Chancellor!

While listening to this song in the winter of 1960, the diarist was struck by a revelation:

> As I gazed at the painted figure singing on the stage to an engrossed audience, wondering so deeply over life that suddenly the man no longer seemed real, nor the theatre,

or the audience; and as I watched that visual thing we call life, there came in a flash to my mind a universal truth, a fairly simple & obvious explanation of the purpose of life, & what it is which makes this life transitory, together with all its little simple delights & sorrows . . .

I looked up from my train seat with a sob and watched the fens itching in the summer heat. The landscape here is as flat as a page. The trees and tracks through the peaty fields are hand-writing. The Isle of Ely and its cathedral spire are where the writer has splodged her pen, got angry and broken up the fibres of earth. The river, where she has found her rhythm again.

Was this 'I's Great Project: the meaning of life? Did she want to be able to answer such questions as why Henry VIII liked boiling heads; why the sanctimonious, self-aggrandising Thomas More wanted to be boiled; why all his bones, except his skull, had been lost; why the diaries had been thrown away; why the diarist had been given so much hope and endured so much failure; why Richard was strapped to a wheelchair, with brain damage; why Dido was dying? Had the diarist detected something during the Lord Chancellor's ridiculous song that could make sense of this relentless destruction? Had she spent the next four and a half million words explaining it?

Mastering my emotion, I returned to the book to find out what this 'flash' of 'universal truth' that she had witnessed could possibly have been:

momentary metaphysical insight but the passed was gone.

but the momentary metaphysical insight passed & was gone.

# 10 Ancestors

Must tell E about how distinguished my family is.

**Aged nineteen**

The first thing every biographer needs when he's trying to make sense of 148 notebooks is another notebook.

How do you begin to catalogue five million words of anonymous writing? In the sticky-bits section of W.H. Smith I picked up Post-it notes. Among the computer software packages, I selected a docket for voice-recognition software. It would take only a few years to read in the entire 15,000 pages. In the hardware department, I changed my mind again. Delighted by the £40 photocopiers, I hoisted one to the check-out; I would do my editing on a duplicate of the books – now I'd have thirty thousand pages. Everything I thought of seemed to involve either damaging the books, or producing so much preparatory work that I'd be dead before I began.

In the end I bought a packet of highlighter pens.

Back at home, I categorised information into five types, one to each radioactive tint of my new highlighters: blue, for physical descriptions:

Mother says I look like a sick ostrich.

Orange, for biographical information:

I have some sort of inkling that I might have been
at the Coliseum in Rome, in a former life.

Pink, for names: Nizzy; Sweet Swoo' Boodies; an art student
called Wolffsky who never – 'gnash!' – becomes her lover; his
rival, who goes by the name of only 'E'; Boots; Humfee; sisters
Noon, Woill and Kate, aka 'that perfectly repulsive child' . . .
Green highlighter was for examples of particularly good
writing and quotable text:

Went out to the library & Backs, sketched St John's bridge
on a Cambridge evening. Homesick for Cambridge even
whilst I'm still in it – the leaf-lit path in John's – a pattern
of shade & sun all down the long wide walk, like a fantasy;
walked with my head in green leaves & my feet on gold.

My diary-writing rather like a form of prayer –
do not pray, but of that temperament – confide
on paper, & get strength from it, it purifies my soul.
It is auto-suggestion, like prayer.

If I die, I will leave countless of these little diaries,
full of heartbreak.

And yellow, for anecdotes:

March, 1959: Archbishop Ramsey gets into her bed.
March, 1960: The second knife attack.
July, 1961: Feeding employer's best cut of lamb to the dog.

I imagined this multicoloured approach would be like
extracting a body from an Irish bog, using neon highlighter
instead of a shovel. I pictured the books laid out in the British

Museum, a hundred years from now: Forensic Biography
Began Here! Author Excavated Subject Using Staedtler Pens!

Behind, stretching into the penumbra would be the
annotated diaries, glowing like fuel rods . . .

Picking out a small memo book, dated 1961, I made
immediate progress with blue (physical description) and green
(quotable):

> A note on my hair – it is glorious, tremendously thick,
> shining in rich goldy & reddy-brown & dark lights –
> prodigality of Nature for my youth, it won't last forever.
> 'Beauty that must die.'

And on a sheet of blank paper, I began a portrait:

which looks like the silhouette of an East End boxer glowering out of a wig. There is no further physical description in the 120 pages of that book. She remains a hairpiece for four years.

> Mr Hely this afternoon – in many ways, I enjoy these visits to the dentist! Enjoy chatting with this kind, feeling man. The treatment was uncomfortable – injections in the vein at the back of the jaw [but] I am so eager to give & receive love, like a desperate little girl, that I got something out of this social contact. Liked his body pressed close to mine, as he sat, & working with his hands on my mouth; the beauty, the tenderness of a man's arms and hands. And feel he likes me, feels the attraction of a girl, with a lot of hair.

In the next book, dated 1963, she is in London at the Camberwell College of Art, working as an artists' model:

> One girl had done a nice sketch of me, & more true to me than a camera. A delicate face, interesting up-slant eyebrows . . .

The sketch isn't included in the diary, and it's impossible to draw delicacy in a face without further information about the nose, so I added just the eyebrows:

'… and light glasses …' continues the entry:

'. . . and the very long bones in my arms, giving me a touch of angularity':

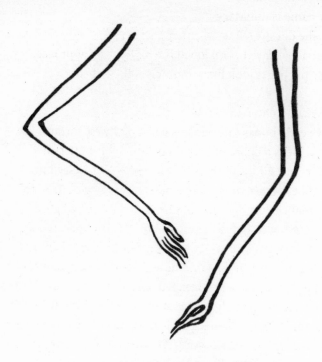

The diary after that, she's in a locker room, 'heart beating fast with expectation', hoping to wrap those bony arms around the etching master, a man called 'J' with 'gorgeous eyes, the eyes of genius' (yellow highlighter: anecdote) – at least, she thinks that's what he's got, because 'am too short sighted to see him well'.

While waiting for him to lunge at her, she hands him a love letter.

But it turns out 'J' doesn't know her first name.

The situation is disintegrating rapidly, so as he accepts the envelope he makes a stab in the dark:

'Mary?' he mutters.

Her name is not Mary.

But she doesn't tell us what her name is.

After a few days I abandoned the highlighter approach. It made the pages look like a municipal flowerbed.


In these early books one name is particularly important: Whiters. He is a figure of yearning, despite his butlerish moniker. 'Just adore Whiters so.' He whips Not-Mary into poetry. She loves Whiters 'like a passion in my blood'. With him, romance 'fills my soul'. But he is also a murky figure. There is no physical description of him. He is clearly manly, yet Not-Mary gives us no sense of his body. To me 'Whiters' suggests somebody in late middle age, barrel-chested, with elegant legs, wearing a dry-cleaned, off-white linen suit. He is a little like my father. The fact that she refers to him by his full nickname, 'Whiters', rather than just 'W', also suggests to me that he is a type of father figure, remote and comfortingly superior, and married. She has known him since she was a very small child.

All the same, only when she is with Whiters does Not-Mary feel fully alive, intense, thrilled to her essence by the thought of what life has to offer her – a life that will be 'dominated' by Art, Beauty and Music. Whiters embodies this mood of radiant potential negatively. He is not an artist. He does not play the piano with thin hands, as does her main boyfriend, 'E'. Whiters' value is that he is a figure of relaxation: he is 'so lovely, so soothing'. Whiters is 'understanding, restful'; Whiters is 'a solace to my irritable, jittery nerves'. In Whiters' presence, the outside world and all that is fretful drop away, and Not-Mary expands into artistry. E (boyfriend number one) is positively artistic, but E is difficult. Whiters is 'joyous'.

Not-Mary appears to be in her early twenties at this period. She is living in bedsits and has no money and, when not thinking about Whiters or E, she is thinking from breakfast to supper about other men.

> Think I am rather a 'sex fiend' just lately – men excite me! Would love to lie in the arms of a man (but with clothes on, think the idea of nudity rather disgusting).

As I was putting one of these early diaries back into the Ribena box, a sheet of blue writing paper dropped onto my duvet. It was small and carefully folded in half, and had created a light indentation in the pages on either side of its hiding place. There was no handwriting. It was blank on both sides. But it was a message from Whiters, all the same: in the left-hand corner at the top, embossed in black in an old-fashioned, self-conscious font, were three lines of an address:

> *Whitefield*
> *Hinton Way*
> *Great Shelford*

'Whiters' is Whitefield: not a lover, but a house.

'No! Not there, love!'
   'Take a plastic bag to sit on if you go in there, darling!'
   'That's the . . . B . . . F . . . I.'
   'The British Film Institute.'
   'Booths For you know what, more like! Two residents' permits, did you say? No, you can't have that . . .'
   I was at the parking permit desk on the top floor of the Cambridge Public Library, trying to find my way to the local history section.

'Last week,' whispered the woman behind the nearest counter, 'when the staff went in to get them out, the man refused to stop! The door you want, love, is over there, on the left.'

The Cambridge Public Library is busier and more fun than the University Library, half a mile away. It is open to everyone and satisfies every need, except privacy. School children mumble intimately down their mobile phones. Foreign students make pingy noises with electronic products. Mothers repack their shopping while their children shoot each other among the DVDs. There is only one place where silence reigns: the Cambridgeshire Collection, set apart from the bustle in a bright room behind a bank-vault door. The tables inside are broad and glossy. There are display cabinets exhibiting pamphlets by famous Cantabrigians who have nothing to do with the university, and a collection of clippings about the 1956 flood. There are also three sets of metal shelves containing small, decaying telephone directories. Otherwise, few books and fewer readers. The place has the feel of a doctor's waiting room, when you've arrived on the wrong day.

'How can I help?' said a sharp voice from behind a computer screen, which turned into a woman's face as I entered. The computer made a gentle whirr. There was a pleasant hum of strip lighting, and from somewhere a suggestion of an open window letting in the summer air.

I handed across my sheet of blue letter paper with the Whitefield address.

'Great Shelford, yes, mmmm . . . Hinton Way,' said the woman's face. A tall body appeared under it, and walked with pronounced steps across the carpet tiles to the telephone directories, reached over the top of the books and tapped at one from behind to nudge it out. 'And who lived at this address?'

'I don't know. Well, I call her Not-Mary, because she's not called Mary. I don't want to know her name, in fact. If you find her name, would you mind covering it up?'

The librarian stopped tapping, considered me thoughtfully and without surprise, and moved six books to the right.

'When did she live there? Or is that another thing you don't want to know?'

'I don't know that she did live there. Maybe she just stole letter paper from there. That would explain why she kept this blank sheet – a sort of trophy. The writer doesn't give her name or home address. She's just "I", who lives . . . "I", who might be anybody,' I added portentously.

The librarian stepped around and behind me, because I was the only real obstacle between her and the facts, and reached down for a third book, riffled the pages, nodded at one in particular, and hurried away.

'The diary I found the paper in was dated 1962,' I called after her.

The Readers' Room of the Cambridgeshire Collection is not where the research material is kept. The proper archive is behind the librarian's desk, past a set of swing doors in the Cavern of Documents.

Twenty minutes later, the librarian returned carrying a thick folder. She let it slide down her forearm and wallop onto my table. In her other hand she held a thin booklet, which she handed to me.

'That's what you need to read first to solve your mystery. It begins four hundred million years ago.'

It was entitled *Whitefield, Hinton Way, Great Shelford: An Archaeological Evaluation*.

*

Four hundred million years ago, Britain was covered by a shallow ocean. The Peak District was an archipelago of islands. Snowdonia had the climate of Hawaii. Everywhere, this mass of water was filled with ammonites the size of small cars. Then the volcanic arrival of Iceland pushed Scotland up in the air; Africa crashed into the Mediterranean and Britain became dry and rippled. Whitefield got its name because it sits on a ripple that is made of old shellfish. At the back of the house is a disused quarry, where the clunch – a poor-quality limestone – was dug out to supply building materials for the field workers' cottages in nearby Shelford.

Whitefield House is one of the most expensive properties in Cambridge.

It's so exclusive, it's invisible. The chunky Cambridgeshire Collection folder contains a sales brochure from 1974 which reveals that the property has an indoor swimming pool, a conservatory, a 'games room', an entrance lobby, a clunky attempt at a baronial staircase, a library, eight bedrooms, and is decorated throughout in pop-star green and silver. The drive leading up to the house runs for a quarter of a mile through an avenue of limes. The building sits on top of a hill, in the middle of twenty-four acres of woodland, just to the south of Cambridge. If it weren't blinded by the trees that surround it, it would have a stunning view. Look out of the train as you pull away from Shelford station to begin the final surge into Cambridge and you can briefly spot the delicious place, disappearing behind you: it's about halfway up the right-hand window, an uneven canopy of oaks and cigar-shaped specimen trees that push above the leaves like Gherkin Towers. Nothing of the house can be seen. Whitefield House isn't listed in the modern telephone directory; it's too posh to hear as well as to see. The fancy foliage sits morose and fat on top of the hill. It's a suitable place for a retired Prime Minister.

The fields to the left of the woodland slope gracefully down, and up again – another copse here, with two houses cut back into the trees – and down, alongside the train tracks to the incinerator tower of Addenbrooke's Hospital.

After that, with a thud, Cambridge.

'You've found yourself a proper mystery here,' said the archivist. 'Your woman may have been thrown in a skip after she died, but if this place is anything to do with her, she certainly didn't begin that way.'

When I got back from the library I sent a postcard to Whitefield House. There was no reply. Two weeks later, driving back from London and slightly irritated, I decided to call unannounced. I pulled off the motorway and drove along the old London road that runs into Cambridge from Linton, the village where my parents first rented a house when they arrived in England in 1966. I was in the mood for ancestors.

As you approach the city from this side, it's a surprise to discover that it is made from trees. Recognisable buildings – the University Library tower, the chapel spires of King's and Jesus, the hump of the Anglo-Saxon castle in the north of the city – emerge from the canopy like islands.

In the far distance I could just make out the tower of my own college, St Edmund's, where I had gone as a distinctly second-rate mathematics student, as a graduate. It was where I first met Dido, and next-door to where she and Richard had discovered the diaries.

The ridge supporting Whitefield is south of Cambridge. A quarter of a mile before you hit the city, a road turns left along Hinton Way. It rises gently, cutting a diagonal slice past a row of furtive bungalows that look as though they're slouching up to the woods for a booze-up. I pulled over beside a farm gate. I was only a few hundred yards from Whitefield House.

It was still invisible.

All her life, the diarist was haunted by these trees and the happy memories they enclosed. I now understood that it was her family home hidden in there in the wood, not merely a place that she stole from. Among those enclosing acres of foliage were Uncle Uke 'playing birdsongs on the gramophone', extensive lawns with 'many rain-pearls of all colours', and pretty Auntie Doll with her weedkiller and secateurs marching up to the dahlia beds in the 'boxie day-night'. An Abyssinia of joys!

Out where I was standing, nothing of the house was apparent. Not a single sign. The corn in the field beside me creaked in the heat.

A stray businessman thundered past in his Audi, smirking because he had discovered yet another short-cut to the Science Park.

It took me half an hour to find Whitefield. I drove slowly through the woods, past various stockbroker-style new-builds squashed in among the beeches. I couldn't spot an entrance. I was beginning to think that the house must be *truly* enormous if it needed this much forestry, when the trees ended and the hill dropped down to Great Shelford. I doubled back, parked beside the farm gate again and walked along the eastern edge of the plot, where the trees were planted as densely as hairbrush bristles. If you live in Cambridge, there's a one in three chance you will one day get a good look at this side of Not-Mary's former property: it is the view from the Addenbrooke's in-patients' oncology ward.

But still I couldn't see a way in.

It was only when I tried the road a third time that I

discovered what I'd missed: two cracked walls curving up through the ivy and undergrowth to a pair of misaligned iron gates. A paper notice from St John's College was stapled to a tree trunk alongside: PRIVATE, DANGER, KEEP OUT.

Behind the metalwork, what had once been Not-Mary's front drive up to Whitefield, the 'house of dreams', collapsed into a rivulet of tarmac among the weeds.

# 11  It was easy to get in . . .

The irony of it – that I should be born into
circumstances like that.
**Aged sixty-one**

It was easy to get in. The wire mesh security panels on
either side of the house gates extended only a few yards,
after which the brambles took over. Bending over and
sticking my bottom out, I pushed my way through the
undergrowth backwards.

The atmosphere was different among the trees: thinner
and unsteady. The sun fluttered around the floor of the wood,
giving it a feeling of playfulness; the weeds were enjoying
their destruction of Not-Mary's front drive.

> Adore the lightness of leaves in space, or anything
> which is lightly fashioned out of air with air again all
> round, like the twig of a tree, or blossoms tip-toe on
> a stem.

Remnants of roadway appeared in gaps of ground elder,
and then, close to where I was standing, the drive forked
into two prongs. The left-hand one was stopped up by a
bank of earth, but the right-hand prong passed alongside
an unexpected field, as though the wood had pinched an
oblong of good arable from a farm and hidden it in here to

wait for the ransom payment. Then the way was blocked by a purple buddleia with spider branches crawling out of a hole in the macadam. On the other side of the buddleia were the remains of the clunch quarry. A fence that had once protected visitors from the edge of this great pit had been pulled down by nettles. Inside, wild shrubs burst from the rockface; roots exploded out of crevices, writhing and twisting, and shot away in fans of elderflower. Massive beeches blocked off the sky. I clambered down to the quarry floor, disturbing a crazed-looking bird that looped off among the leaves. The air down there was fastened in by tendrils. 'A fairy glade', Not-Mary calls it, 'ethereal with the sunlight through the leaves . . . remote, misty, not real'.

From the quarry a dirt track led back into the main wood, which quickly opened out into a large, overgrown patch of grass, perhaps a lawn, next to which was a hillock, which I climbed.

Overhead, a small aeroplane passed across the gap between the treetops, and from where I stood among the trees looking out, it felt as if the pilot was searching for surviving communities after a war. Not-Mary mentions these planes as happy occurrences. They emphasised Whitefield as a retreat from the world's 'frenzy', a woodland enclave separate from 'reality', a burrow of 'dreaming', a 'paradise on earth', the only place where 'I feel spiritual and uplifted'.

But there was still the question of the house. I couldn't spot it. Two storeys, gabled roofs, eight bedrooms, a fourteen-foot-high ballroom, library, orangery and a proportionate number of chimneys on top. Not an easy thing to miss. Baffled, I began to clamber back down from my vantage point and, looking at my feet to take care around the various strange potholes in the earth, I suddenly understood. I knew where Whitefield was. I was standing on it. My hillock was a mound of rotting bricks.

*The Piano Room at Whitefield:* I played my own tunes with great abandonment & enjoyment, & in the beauty of my own musicality. And with purified soul, thoroughly enjoyed all the rest of the evening.

*The Lawn, facing the Orangery:* Dreamt E and I were among roses – a lot of green prickly leaves, & the roses of all colours, yellow, red, etc. Yet at the same time the rose bushes were what I was wearing – my hair, my shirt. E was ticking me off rather, & telling me I should have them cut shorter . . . and next dreamt I was lying on the lawn, and screaming protest, my head on a pair of shears, and my hands gripping the handles but my protest was not greatly in earnest. I liked it really. And E angrily cut away at the roses on me, cut my shirt shorter.

*The Maids' Toilet?*: Times of deep magic, unaccountable . . . in that cell-like maids' wickery, shelter of dreams, with the wind in the pines outside, and light and shadow across the white-washed wall. A wonderful dreaming place . . . half wished it were my prison.

*The Drawing Room*: A very nice day, being happy & well, and enjoying the jokes. Nice lunch. After lunch when music was on the wireless, felt the true, deep, creative mood come over me.

71

## 12  Two close shaves

Quick kiss of E in doorway, a taken kiss.
**Aged nineteen**

'The diarist I told you about?' I whispered the next time I
stepped into the Cambridgeshire Collection room. It was
the same efficient female behind a computer screen who'd
brought me the Whitefield House folder two weeks earlier.
'I've unearthed something new, an astonishing coincidence:
she used to work here! Yes, the woman who wasn't called
Mary whose address I don't want to know was a temporary
librarian for six months *here*, in Cambridge Public Library!'

The librarian's friendly face popped out above the VDU just
as before. For a moment it jiggled there. She looked a little
strained, I thought. The absence of readers was perhaps
particularly exhausting that day. Then she disappeared from
view again, re-emerged on the right of the screen and leaned
forward, intrigued.

I'd hoped to be able to write this biography in a correct
chronological sequence: first Not-Mary's ancestors (starting
four hundred million years ago with the ammonites), followed
by her birth, her schooling, her adulthood, including answers
to the great questions in order of emotive importance (What
was her 'immortal' project? Who was the Peter whom she
describes as her 'gaoler' in the later books? Why were the
diaries thrown out?) – all this somehow without learning her

name, which would appear for the first and only time on the final page, as in a Gothic short story, with a photo of her gravestone. The world's first biography of a nameless subject would follow the same pattern as a biography of Einstein.

But vile 'information' kept popping up – clues about new ways to discover the writer's identity that threatened to destroy everything, but which I couldn't ignore.

It was my own fault. I should have locked myself in my study for five years like a proper scholar. Instead, each time I hit a fresh lead I jumped up and rushed into the undergrowth on the tops of hills. Now here I was again, putting the project at risk of a solution. 'See?' I said, pressing open a little black rexine notebook.

> A library day again. What a work-a-day world this is –
> hard, cold fact of work to do, endless 'overdues'.
> Feeling very much in love with <u>sweet</u> little darling E . . .

'That's *this* library she's talking about. She got a post here in 1958. And here's another one, when she was also staffing some of the village branches':

> A chilly hall (though modern. Has less books than
> Trumpington, and thoroughly common & brainless
> people) . . .

'But she has lots of nice things to say too,' I added hurriedly:

> Jan. 22: today absolutely intoxicated with joy;
> a wonderful day of deep magic . . . My library day
> a real treat. Enjoy shelving – feel how shelving
> books around the library gives me a deep feeling
> of librarianship & how it suits my personality –

a feeling of being cultured, serious, sensitive and intellectual. Jolly Swerbles, the sweep of the counter with the books, & those great big carry trays.

'She loved it so much, she was going to take librarian exams':

Jan. 26: Feel that I am born to librarianship, and pride in it as a profession. Got a nice compliment today – one of the readers said Johnny [the head librarian] said I am 'one of the intelligent ones.' Must keep up this enthusiasm by perseverance, & get somewhere in life – what could make one happier than success?

'And then three days later you sacked her. See, here':

Thursday Jan 29th: **Lost my post** – and thus, like a house of cards, the complete collapse of all I have – my lovely post, career as a librarian with Cambridge City Libraries, my independence. Feel really afraid of life now . . .

'Fifty years ago she probably had your job. You have all the facts about who she is here after all. It's in this building some- where – down in that document cavern of yours. You've had her name in the archives all along.'

It was a tense moment. All this librarian had to do was check the file of past employees to locate 'I's name, at which point my hunt would be over. There was no way, I realised with eager sadness, that I could fail to succeed.

The librarian shook her head and returned to studying her computer screen. 'Sorry. Can't help you. We're not allowed to keep that sort of information, because of Data Protection. Just last week I got rid of fifteen more folders about old employees.

Ironic, isn't it? Here we are, the local history department, and we burn our own.'

I left the library with a sigh of pleasure and walked around the market square three times, perked up by the fact that, when writing a biography, you can't trust certainties. Just as you're about to pounce on something that will condemn you to a tidy answer, poooooofff! It vanishes.


It was during a description of a day in the library that the mysterious figure of E first appears in Not-Mary's diary. In those days, the library was not where it is now, in the city shopping mall, but just off the market square in a building that is now a Jamie Oliver restaurant. In Not-Mary's time the prosciutto counter was the Fiction bay; the ravioli machine, Gardening. On the day that E first appears in the diaries, Not-Mary was nineteen years old and stamping books in the middle of a basket of tomatoes waiting to be made into 'Cilindretti Pasta Pillows'.

Feeling 'strangely excited, and very hot' because she'd just spotted a 'swerb picture of John Gielgud – curling hair, side view' in a picture book about Peggy Ashcroft – she looked up from her stamping desk and there it was: the letter E, standing in front of her, at the head of the queue.

> I gave the usual terrific jump I do at the sight of E unexpectedly, & sat down on the chair.

'You're a funny girl,' said E when Not-Mary had recovered from his unexpected appearance. He didn't leave the library after that; he wandered around, out of sight, keeping Not-Mary's heart pounding. Not-Mary describes him as a 'little' person, Jewish, with at one time 'intense, blue eyes' and at another 'vivid' brown eyes, and 'manly hands' which she calls 'knobbly' when she's cross. He has a foreign accent, possibly German or Austrian. Although he never steps out from behind the capital letter E to give us his name, between the second volume of the diaries in 1958 and the books of the early 1980s, there is not a single volume in which Not-Mary mentions E fewer than 350 times. In the early books she quotes his sayings with hypnotic loyalty:

> E said I am exceptionally pretty.
> E said Florence [the city] smells.
> E said the period is a great handicap and burden to a woman, a dreadful thing and unnecessary.
> E said Men have their troubles too, eg the bother of shaving.

E believes that genius in Art is the greatest attainment of mankind, Beethoven's 4th Piano Concerto is the summit of that lofty pinnacle, and acknowledges sweetly (if you press him) that he has himself published a few poems. In the 1950s and 1960s Not-Mary records a total of sixty or seventy pages of his pronouncements, each beginning 'E said . . .'

Sometimes he expands his lungs and emits five pages of Esaids in one puff:

> E said I must work, work, work.
> E said it is no good crying.
> E said I should stay up all night if necessary to get my work done.
> E said it not all depressing, to the contrary.

E appeared twice in front of Not-Mary on that day in the library. The second time, he came back holding a book. What would his choice be? Rilke's *Duino Elegies*? *Bach and the Meaning of Counterpoint*? Volume Two of *Study and Criticism of Italian Art*?

No. As he reached the front of the queue, he gave Not-Mary a 'mischievous smile'. It was *English Villages in Colour*.

E knew how to enjoy himself as well as the next man.

After she was sacked from the library, Not-Mary had to fill in application forms to get another job, and these included a question about her education:

> Have said I was at the Perse School for Girls in Cambridge. I should not really tell such things, it is bad for the reputation of the Perse.

I hated to do it, but I called them. It was possible that they would be able to tell me who Not-Mary was.

One of the best secondary schools in England, the Perse School for Girls (now called the Stephen Perse Foundation) is hidden in a genteel sector of the city close to the University Botanical Gardens. It is pressed in by macaroon houses, the smallest of which costs half a million pounds; Not-Mary calls the area a 'slum'.

There is a large quantity of school squeezed behind these houses, but the way in is disguised to look like a tradesmen's entrance. Through this unassuming side door the world opens large. Posters in the lobby show splendid young females playing football; begoggled young females surrounded by chemistry retorts; bronzed young females with furrowed brows helping Africans with water-based projects. Among the posters, corridors scuttle off to different parts of the school.

'Have you nothing else to go on apart from the fact that she was not Mary?' asked an amused woman named Catherine, who stepped out of one of these tunnels to greet me. She was the school librarian and archivist.

'Oh, yes,' I said. 'I know a lot more than that. I know that she was here from 1957 to 1959, and I know that she wasn't called Mary because she didn't seduce a man at Luton College of Art.'

For a few seconds the librarian and I were in open air, beside what appeared to be a small park. 'Amanda!' shouted Catherine as we passed a line of girls carrying sports shoes, 'Mary Beard's *The Parthenon* is back. I have set it aside for you.'

We hurried down a ramp and passed alongside a large refectory hall. 'But you cannot have it,' Catherine called again, remembering, 'until you have returned Simone de Beauvoir.'

'The archive is slightly disordered, I'm afraid . . .' she said when we reached a dim room filled with misshapen cupboards and display cabinets. She stooped inside and immediately began blowing dust off old reports, lifting aside architects' models for new classrooms and grimacing behind a framed poster advertising a performance of *The Oresteia*. Within minutes she was halfway round the room.

For almost an hour this enthusiastic, kind woman and I riffled among the clutter. But there was nothing. No appropriate list of previous pupils that included one living at Whitefield. Nothing in the alumni catalogue suggested an Old Persean who had set out from the school for a future in painting, determined to master an 'immortal' project that would one day leave the world gasping at her legacy; no record of fundraising packs sent care of a man called Peter whom she describes as her 'gaoler'.

Then abruptly Catherine let out a cry of triumph. 'Is this,

perhaps, a photograph of the woman you are looking for?'

And, undoubtedly, it was.

But it was also a picture of seventy-two other unnamed people. It was the school photo of 1957.

# 13  Birth

> Am coming to the daily increasing opinion that
> I am born an artist, an artist in whatever medium
> I choose to create . . .
>
> **Aged twenty-one**

'Whooooooaaah! The first thought I had when I saw this handwriting? I thought: Nameless Person, whoever you are, I don't want to be in the same room as you.'

Barbara Weaver, chairwoman of the Association of Qualified Graphologists, laid the diary I'd given her onto the dining-room table and studied it from behind her thin glasses with looming hazel eyes. She was wearing a brown blouse that was halfway to becoming a kaftan. Dropping from her chair, she sped voleishly from the room – then sped back carrying a magnifying lens the size of a breadboard.

'Yes, that's the first thing I'd think,' she resumed with a contented shuffle of her hips as she sat down again. 'The person who has handwriting like this is a complete nutter.'

Barbara is also principal of the Cambridge School of Graphology ('Though when I say "school", there's really only me'), and runs all her business from a converted set of barns in a village just north of Cambridge called Landbeach. We were sitting in her Sunday dining room. The mahogany table shimmered with polish. The light-blue carpet glowered with suspicion that I was about to drop a blob from my coffee mug. The next village along from Barbara's is Waterbeach, where the subject of my first book had lived: Stuart Shorter. Not many people had wanted to be in the same room with him, either.

Barbara dug out a plastic ruler from the mound of pencils and protractors she'd dumped beside her on the table, balanced the breadboard magnifier against her bosom at the same angle that sunbathing actresses put mirrors, and leaned over the page excitedly. 'Ooooooh, look at those mid-zones . . .'

Diaries are terrible liars. They record dramas out of context, encourage paranoia, rearrange facts, are deliberately biased and self-justifying, blind you with irrelevance, censor alternative opinion, exaggerate petty complaints into tragic emblems and, in particular, wallow in the fact that any fool can write about dejection, but describing happiness takes determination and skill. Most diaries are moans in writing, even when the person writing them is happy.

I'd come across Barbara on the web. She has an old-fashioned site, like a parish magazine, with columns and boxed inserts and a tone of suppressed gossip. 'Psychoanalysis by biro', boasts her home page. 'My sister and I were frankly astonished at how accurate your findings were,' write 'identical twins' M and L ('names withheld for privacy purposes'). 'Our husbands read them' and 'they thought the same. Some of your findings caused heated debate and quite a bit of soul searching.'

Beneath a specimen of script in which the closing letter of each word throws up its final stroke like a girl flinging up her skirts in a village pub, Barbara has written stiffly: 'Desire for attention.' Not-Mary's words do not end like this. Her words appear to be squeezing along drains. Not-Mary, as the later books make clear, has a desire for disappearance.

In another specimen of peculiar script, Barbara has high-lighted the writer's 'd's and 't's. The up and down strokes of the vertical line of the 't's make a distinct 'tent' shape.

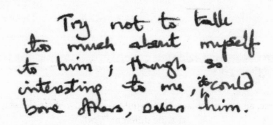

Next weekend could be a bit hectic. I tried to write to Dad but he was spending the day

'Stubbornness,' declares Barbara.

Not-Mary's 'd's are quite different, like Greek deltas. They're 'd's that have been slapped across the back of the neck.

Click 'Services' on Barbara's website and you see an excerpt from a handwritten note by a mother who has secretly sent in a portion of her daughter's handwriting. Barbara doesn't pull her punches. She says nothing about the daughter's script; she picks out the 'tangled lines' of the mother's note. 'Confusion of interests,' she pronounces decisively. In another example, deceit is revealed by the letters 'a' and 'o'. Instead of the line that completes these vowels running over the top, as usual, it loops inside it, as though the devious writer had snatched down a telephone cable and were winding it greedily through the kitchen window. Not-Mary's letters are never like this.

I'd given Barbara three books: one from the 1960s, when Not-Mary's hand bounced across the page at four words to the line:

Try not to talk too much about myself to him ; though so interesting to me, it could bore others, even him.

One, from 1979, when the writing first begins to look like a line of bugs:

> Went on foot to town this afternoon — A number of people about. Somehow, I felt afraid of every group of ruffians or layabouts I saw, wondering if they were strikers, or people laid off. One day they will knock me down, and run off with the groceries or goods I have bought. It only needs the police to strike next

And one of the brilliantly-coloured books, from 2001. It was this last that had shocked Barbara. Somewhere between the origin of words in Not-Mary's brain and their appearance at the end of her pen, her thoughts have turned into worms: tiny, wriggling and innumerable. As I looked at the pages again over Barbara's shoulder, I absorbed some of her analytic spirit. This, I thought with a shock, is the handwriting of somebody getting herself ready to be thrown out in a skip.

Of course, all my own plans in my youth were just a pie in the sky, as I have a quite different "God"

'It's not her eyesight that's making this so small,' pronounced Barbara, making a note on a jotting pad. 'She's not got especially bad eyesight, or else she'd get tired before she could write this much. Alzheimer's is also associated with small letters, but this person remembers everything, so it's not that . . .' Barbara squinted into mid-air as if the outline of Not-Mary was starting to take shape there, quickly added another word to her pad, and dropped her head back to the magnifier.

Graphologists believe that the central nervous system is directly linked to the emotions, and therefore minute impulses in the brain cause individual variations to handwriting that can be reliably related to character. Crudely put, the interpretative idea is that if you can determine what an average and unremarkable hand looks like, then a person's abnormal character traits will be determined by the ways in which their writing deviates from the bland middle ground.

To help simplify analysis, graphologists divide a person's script into three zones: upper, middle and lower. The 'upper zone' is the high space occupied by the tall letters: this zone represents intellectual and spiritual matters – the extension of the everyday into the realm of ideals and dreams. Bill Gates' handwriting has a large upper zone:

may you make billions someday

Britney Spears' has a little one:

I want to apologize for the
past incedent with the umbrella.

I want to apologize for the
past incedent with the umbrella.

Not-Mary's upper zone is large.

The 'lower zone' is the space under the bulk of the word, where the dangly segments of 'g' and 'p' grope about. This zone reveals the writer's instincts, activities and motivation; it shows, according to Barbara, 'how a person feels about money, possessions and the powers of her body.' One of Barbara's website links opens a window with a scan of a letter by Stewart Blackburn. 'Handwriting of a murderer', chirrups the headline. The case is repulsive. Blackburn killed his girlfriend by setting light to her then locking her in a room. The extract is from a letter he wrote to the woman's parents after he was convicted. His 'y's have a very distinctive lower zone:

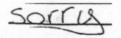

'The extreme leftward trend', observes Barbara, shows he has 'unresolved issues' with his mother or 'mother substitute'. Not-

Mary (particularly in the colourful books) writes her 'y's and 'g's in a similar way:

I went on with the book on "Dennis Neilson", as I couldn't sleep
It seems he was very good at English literature, and was a good writer;
I might think he could have been a novelist, if he hadn't
turned to murdering.

The 'middle zone' of handwriting is everything in between the high bits of a 'd' and the low bits of a 'y': it is the majority of the text. An average hand uses roughly 3mm for each zone. Much more or less, or in different proportions, and Barbara's glasses quiver on her nose. For a perfectly average person, you'd expect the distance from the top of the letter 't' to the bottom of 'p' to be about 9mm.

For the diarist of the third book it is 2mm.

'But analysis is not just about letter shape; it cannot be that simplistic,' insisted Barbara. She raised the diary above her head to catch the light against some pressure marks that had caught her interest, turned the page over to check the other side, and began to speak with the clipped specificity of a police investigator: 'Writing does not leave any evident indentations on the back of the paper . . . energy levels not high . . . experiences wash over writer, leaving little impression . . . doesn't learn from past mistakes . . .'

Barbara broke off and looked up with a startled smile.

'You need to look at the writing as a whole. Only when you've studied everything, including the way sentences relate to each other on the page, can you make a proper assessment. Just this morning I was reading one expert who claimed that if you write "g"s like this . . .

. . . then you're a lesbian. That little bow at the bottom, like a lasso-y loop, is supposedly a guilt sign, because you're coming back. But I've seen loads of gay men who do their "g"s that way; there is male and female in everyone . . . AhhgggHHH! Don't put that cup there!' She skimmed a coaster across the din-ing-table polish; it came to rest under my mug. 'My husband did that just after he made this table. One sip and off he had to go, strip the wood down and start over again.'


Graphologists peddle fantastic certitudes when all they have is guesswork and a sense of theatre–that's what I had thought before I met Barbara: they're hucksters. They've hucksted them-selves first, and now they're out to huckst you. 'They remind me of someone,' I'd said to myself as I drove to this meeting in Landbeach. 'That's right, that's who: they're exactly like biographers. They remind me of me!' They use the same sort of language as biographers; they operate with the same vague sense of self-importance that they are pursuers of 'truth', which means, in other words, that they like to hear themselves be opinionated; they are driven by the same gossipy curiosity. Put two graphologists (or biographers) in a room together and they can scarcely agree on each other's name.

I like the graphologists I've met. A few months earlier I'd been to see Patricia Field, who'd published an article on Jane Austen's handwriting. Patricia, like Barbara, was interested in 'd's. She pointed out the importance of Not-Mary's delta. It is a well-known marker of creativity to write the letter in that way.

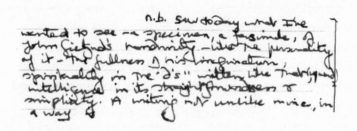

n.b. saw today what I've wanted to see – a specimen, a facsimile,
of John Gielgud's handwriting – like the personality of it –
the fullness of his imagination, spirituality in the "d's" written
like that, (upwind), intelligence in its straightforwardness &
simplicity. A writing not unlike mine, in a way

I agreed contentedly: 'Yes, I do those deltas too.'

'And they can also suggest an excessive desire for attention, perhaps an inferiority complex, people who'll do anything to get noticed.'

When the diarist's 'd's are compared to the rest of the text, Patricia said 'I' was held back by tentativeness and lack of resolve. For all her great artistic urge, Not-Mary might have ended up just a cook.

According to Patricia, the 'm's also suggested that Not-Mary had a closed nature, because of the way this letter was curved at the top, like the arches under railway viaducts. Open people write 'm's with fallen arches, as if two 'u's have been put together. There is a connection, Patricia had said, between 'm' and the way children hold hands when they are playing ring-a-ring-a-roses. Those hatchet-faced kids who keep their knuckles facing upward during this old English dance write their 'm's as Not-Mary does. The saps who clasp from underneath, knuckles down, tend to do the collapsed sort.

Barbara, on the other hand, is much too cautious to be drawn into clear physical statements. She insists it is not possible for graphology even to determine if a writer is male or female. Not-Mary writes the rounded 's', 'which of course means yielding, and as a female you're more likely to compromise and give in. But it would mean the same thing in a man.'

In her expert thirty-page report, produced for the slight sum of £100 after reading the three books I'd brought and studying and comparing the handwriting of each, Barbara concludes that by the end of her life, the diarist

> is in a negative state of mind and is in low spirits most of the time. She is an inveterate worrier and usually expects the worst of people and situations. She is shy and timid, appearing awkward and uncomfortable. She is likely to dress soberly so as not to attract attention [and] she is typically attracted to someone unavailable. Because she feels her parents were inadequate, this also produces a longing for the 'good parent' – the person who will see her as she truly is. In the extreme, emotional breakdown or suicide is likely.

In films, the pathologist – in order to give the contemptuous and disbelieving copper a first approximation of time of death – stands over a slab and performs a post-mortem on the corpse. In biographies of unknown diarists, Barbara Weaver peers down at her mahogany dining table and performs a post-scriptum on the corpus.

The slant of handwriting is a measure of its 'emotional dial'. Barbara looked up sharply, and from her heap of implements plucked out a plastic protractor, its edges dimpled with rulings. Writing that slopes to the right suggests the person is outgoing and confident; straight up and down, an independent spirit; a slant to the left, shyness.

left slant

right slant

'Yes, mmm, a shrinking violet . . . a severe case, inclined to suicide . . . possibly abusing alcohol or drugs . . . a hoarder . . . dejected and melancholic . . . born, let's see, yes, May 22nd, 19 . . . 1939.'

'You can tell from the handwriting?' I burst out, unable to hide my disbelief any longer.

'Oh no!' retorted Barbara, looking up from her breadboard magnifying glass with a delighted smile. 'I can tell that from reading what she's written. Haven't you tried doing that yet?'

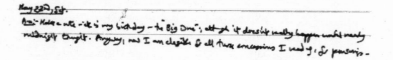

<u>May 22nd, Sat.</u> [1999]
A.m.:– Make a note – it is my birthday –the "Big One"; although it doesn't really happen until nearly midnight tonight. Anyway, now I am eligible for all these concessions I read of, for pensioners.

# 14 A Chapter of celebrations: birthdays from thirteen to sixty-two

**1952** Birthday list

1. fountain pen or biro
2. big pen knife
3. sleeping bag
4. dictionary
5. doll. (boy or girl).
6. cartrige paper drawing book (bla)
7. pastels.
8. ballet shoes.
9. trousers.
10. gun for Henry
11. new white vest for yaby.
12. yolly's tea set.
13. pyjamas. for Henry
14. dressing-gown for Henry.
15. a length of pink ribbon.
16. a party dress.

**AGED THIRTEEN**

**1961** As I expected it was a good birthday. My spirits run high, full of health and youthful optimism. So far, enjoying being 22. Wonder if these are the best years.

AGED TWENTY-TWO

**1962** Just woken from a lovely dream of c-feel –
a birthday treat indeed – a happy dream, for me – one
in which my needs for superiority & social worth are
satisfied. AGED TWENTY-THREE

**1964** Spent my birthday at home. Can't understand it.
I eat well, & don't lose an undue amount of blood.
Does every woman feel the period so much, in terms
of strengthlessness and nervous reaction? A whole
bloody week of feeling awful, in every four!

AGED TWENTY-FIVE

**1974** My birthday, and perhaps the most uncelebrated
I ever had!

Had a little eavesdrop, later in the evening, when
Dame Harriette was in the drawing room; having an
uncanny instinct of knowing when I'd be mentioned.
Miss N said I am very happy. She asked D.H. about what
my interests were, & D.H. seemed quite at sea. She said I
watch television 'all the time', which annoyed me, as it is
quite untrue. AGED THIRTY-FIVE

**1975** My birthday, and possibly the quietest ever.
A quiet usual day, and Little Harriette unaware of the
fact – didn't want to worry her about it. But just to have
her still, is present enough – in fact, to have all the old
people. AGED THIRTY-SIX

**1977** My birthday, and a dull one – luckily I don't care.
Really have had enough of the old people. They are such
 a drag.                                                      AGED THIRTY-EIGHT

**1978** My birthday, and I take stock of what received.
Words and love are what I crave, not material things.
The nightie from [my sister] Noon is generous, but not
what I want – I want words.

It is a great comfort that Puddn' [another sister]
thinks that being single is best – she really does. And she
knows. Has had so much experience with men. She says
the attraction wears off, and she agrees that then one is
very unfree and trapped.

E is doubtless too busy dying, inch by inch, to think
of my birthday.

39 is nice to write, from a calligraphic point of view.
                                                      AGED THIRTY-NINE

**1982** My birthday, which fact I keep forgetting, as I've
felt 43 long before now. Read in the paper that Sophia
Loren wants extra luxuries in jail. She is a dreadful
big-headed, spoilt woman. It jolly well serves her right.
Ever so glad to see an over-lucky, very self-satisfied &
healthy person have a little set-back like that. All stuffed
with sleep etc.                                          AGED FORTY-THREE

**1983** Having had a good night, I remembered it is my
birthday. Weigh in at 10st. 6lbs.    AGED FORTY-FOUR

**1984** It sounds as if I nearly died when I was born,
because they couldn't cope with the mucus new babies
get – I was even christened when I was just born, & had

the last sacraments. It is a poignant story, because it would have been terrible for Moth & Pa if I had died – their first baby. Wonder if it would have been better if I had died.                                    **AGED FORTY-FIVE**

**1993** Glad to see the back of today.

                                             **AGED FIFTY-FOUR**

**1996** It is my birthday; and I have been a very busy pensioner, it not a day of leisure. The TV had something really good for once – a medical programme, about the latest in heart surgery. The film was about four men who were having a specialist operation; and three of them were over 70. Although it was late, I felt I had to see all the film, as I wanted to find out how the patients did. As it happened, three of them died.

                                             **AGED FIFTY-SEVEN**

**1997** It is my birthday! And I am not very keen about it. I thought how enormous I felt – like a beached whale; and even my breasts seem to have swollen, when that part of me always used to be thin.

                                             **AGED FIFTY-EIGHT**

**1998** Make a note; it is my birthday; and I didn't remember it at first.

   Mother has been abysmal – has sent me £9.

   It seems with these pensioners, their brains give out before their bodies; about the only explanation.

                                             **AGED FIFTY-NINE**

**1999** Make a note – it is my birthday – the 'Big One' . . . Moth told me something that I hadn't known, in the

Botanical Gardens; that my birth was induced, so it was quick, but incredibly uncomfortable. It seems the doctor had wanted to go flying, the next day. And another baby who was born in a similar fashion was given too much oxygen, so was blinded. Myself also trouble with 'mucus', and given oxygen.

It might explain why I am a fearful person.

AGED SIXTY

**2000** Make a note; it is my birthday; rather a gloom falling over my day; yet other people do nice things at my age – like 'Anna Ford' getting married this summer. I have been to Histon Road. When I got back, I found that the can of cider I had bought at the wine shop had sprung a leak. AGED SIXTY-ONE

**2001** Make a note; it is my birthday, of course. I thought Moth looked very old, as she walked away down the drive. It has been quite a good birthday, considering what an awful traumatic year it is; and what will be the situation in a year's time, I wonder.

AGED SIXTY-TWO

## 15 The Oldest book

Read my 1952 diary, & old reports. What a
troublesome creature I was.

**Aged twenty**

The oldest book in the Ribena box is a thin, beige hardback, twenty-three plain pages inside, and made from two slabs of cardboard stuck over with brown parcel paper. The linen spine has once been orange or pink, but it has gone to the bad. On the front cover, inside a large square, is the printed instruction:

## GENERAL EDUCATION
### ROUGH NOTES

A child has been briefly at work around this message, splodging ink and nonsense words. In the bottom right-hand corner a self-contented cursive has filled in the date: '1952'. And underscored it twice, slash! slash!

Inside the book, the handwriting is large and clumsy and crashes about the paper:

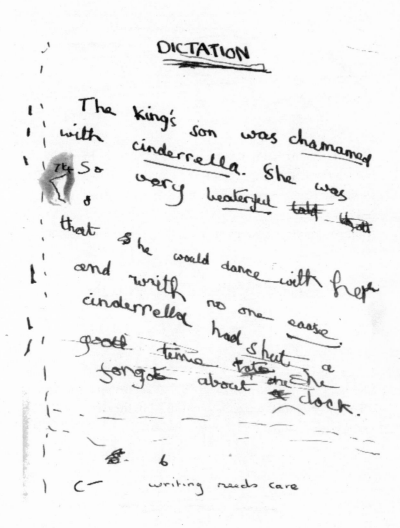

Many of the pages contain drawings, some of which might be by a small boy:

or definitely by a girl:

or a psychotic:

There is some good mathematics:

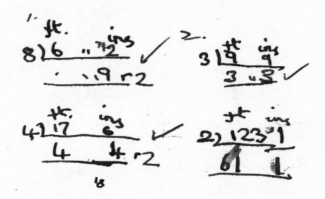

and an invented country called Beano that looks like France and has rivers named after milk products, French intellectuals and abusive words for black people:

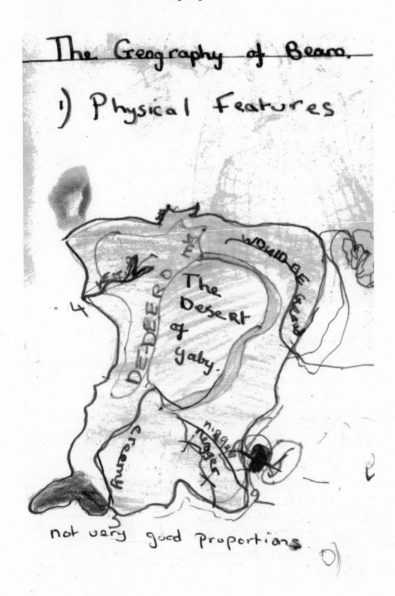

Five of the central pages contain illustrations too faint to reproduce. In almost imperceptible pencil, so delicate that you think for a moment that the real lines are on the other side of the paper, these pictures show a small girl weeping at a piano. She is slumped on her stool, her head sunk in the crook of one arm like one of Charles Dickens' pathetic orphans. There is no face: just hair, limbs and defeat.

Did this book belong to Not-Mary, or did it not? Excited by my detective work, I totted up the 148 volumes in the collection and divided them into eight categories:

1) The set of seven Max-Val exercise books smelling of Ovaltine that contain the cartoon strip.

2) The six red pads with rexine covers, containing the draft of the novel beginning ' "What a beautiful morning!" Clarence hummed and sang under his breath.'

3) This very early exercise book, dated 1952.

4) The books belonging to an early adult phase, in which the writing is tidy, methodical but still outsized and taking up all the space on the page, as if poured in with a watering can.

5) A long period with smaller script that uses office notebooks of two types: Collins 'Red Books', and an unbranded hard-back with a blue marbled cover that looks as though you're staring down at the sea.

6) The lurid-coloured books from the 1990s in which, just by glancing at the pages, not even bothering to read the text, you can tell that something about the author has gone seriously wrong.

7) Four tiny day-to-day pocket diaries, of the sort that have syringe-shaped pencils slotted into the spine.

8) The empty books. This group is especially touching, or shocking, depending on the mood in which you come across them. There are eleven empty books, all different types: an artists' watercolour pad; an address book with letters running up one edge like a staircase; the book with the cheese-mould stripes. I imagine these blank volumes piled on Not-Mary's desk after her death, waiting for a time that would never come. Alternatively, I imagine them scattered all over the room, overlooked in her race to fill up the other volumes.

I felt pleased with myself. I was narrowing in on my subject, using Scotland Yard methods. My trip to Whiters had exposed her ancestry; the graphology visit had resulted, albeit embarrassingly, in her date of birth. As christening follows birth, I next needed to find her name.

In my new gold, Swedish-designed notebook I jotted down a tally of my progress.

*Name?* Anything but Mary.

*Date of Birth?* May 22nd, 1939.

*Siblings?* Three sisters.

*Parents (not a particularly interesting question at the best of times)?* Unknown.

*Subject of her 'great project'?* Unknown. Unlikely to be scientific – no formulae or technological sketches in the books. When very young and looking for work, refuses a job at a library because 'only rotten old science books there'. Science makes her yawn. Exception is medicine. Has read numerous medical textbooks.

*Reasons for failure of project?* Unknown.

*Name of person who pitched her diaries in the skip or their reasons?* Unknown.

*Who E?* Unknown.

I pulled myself up on the pillows of my bed and thought about other things. I wondered if I liked Not-Mary. For all her angry bluster about the world and her situation at the end of her life when she's locked up with the man called Peter whom she wants to strangle and stab, she seems a mild and gentle woman. She has an endearing mix of timidity and lust for life. I remembered a scene, described in an early book, in which she leaves Whitefield wood to cycle to Cambridge. Pedalling nervously down the hill towards Addenbrooke's Hospital (it was one of her terrors that cars were poised at all junctions and driveways to shoot out and mow her over), she had a 'wonderful primitive fantasy'. She imagined escaping into a forest. She would live forever there 'the natural life, close to the earth, and what is more in the deepest, darkest, windiest depths of the wood', and 'lie with some sweet creature in my arms – my lover'.

She had, she appends primly to this extract, 'no physical desire for sex' with this man, 'just spiritual desire . . .'

But then, for the first time in her remarks about sex, she hesitates.

The night hurtling past her ears, the softness of flesh, the still-felt warmth of that bath she'd just had at Whitefield . . .

'Imagine sex would be tremendously exciting,' she adds.

At Long Road cattery she redoubled her grip on the handlebars, flung out her legs and, her thoughts thrilling, coasted into Cambridge 'soap-scented'.

\*

It was in the middle of the night that I got it. That was what was wrong!

The book from 1952, with the childish doodles inside, was too thin.

What notebook contains only twenty-three pages?

I barely had to move my hand to pick the spindly thing up again, and I now felt the front covers slither awkwardly across the pages inside. Flipping the board back, I saw, very close to the spine, that two-thirds of the pages had been removed.

Hurrying out of my bedroom to my study, I returned with a magnifying glass.

Removed, I decided with a gasp of excitement, using a razor.

# 16  Vince, private detective

Interview with private detective Vincent Johnson.

*Location:* CB2 Café, Cambridge

*Dates:* March 12th, 2012; April 14th, 2015

AM:    Sections of this interview are being recorded. Do you mind?

VJ:    No.

AM:    The purpose of the recorder, when I use it, is not to stitch you up. It's so that I can be sure to keep an accurate record of what you say.

VJ:    I understand.

AM:    As with all people I interview for this book, you can check the copy before it goes in.

VJ:    *(Amused)* Alexander, I'm not worried. I know where you live.

AM:    Is it all right to call you Vince?

VJ:    Yes.

AM:    Vince, please explain what you do.

Even in the murky back room of the café, Vince has a look of alarming consequence. He seems to be covered in bark, not skin. When he reaches across the table to shake your hand, it's as if he's bringing a large branch around the side of a tree trunk.

VJ: I am a private investigator and founder director of the Cambridge Detective Agency, which manages surveillance, process serving, tracing, divorce, missing persons and a whole spectrum of criminal defence cases, which range from petty theft to murder. Most of what we do is very mundane. Frequently we do something dangerous, but occasionally we do something bizarre. In the thirty years I have been running the company, we have investigated over twenty thousand cases. Before that, I was the youngest serving CID officer in the Cambridgeshire constabulary.

AM: How did you become a detective?

VJ: As a young policeman, I lived above the police station. When I was bored and as I was new to the area I used to go down to the collator's office, which was the intelligence centre of the station, and memorise the photographs of the villains, and also their address, the postcode, who their associates were, what car they drove, the registration number. I believe I met the subject of your previous biography on several occasions.

AM: Stuart Shorter?

VJ: Nice lad.*

*As Vince later explained in an email: 'During the course of an interview with him – he was not a suspect, it was an enquiry about another matter to do with homelessness – he remarked upon my waterproof jacket, which was a Drizabone. He said that he would love one to keep him warm and dry on the streets. I did not say anything at the time to him because I was a bit embarrassed, but I did remember it and about 2 months later I found this same chap sitting in the rain in Sidney Street. I took my jacket off and put it round his shoulders and then walked on. Didn't think anything of it because it was most probably one of the better spontaneous things I have done.'

[In 2012 Vince was voted ABI Investigator of the Year for his work on a missing persons inquiry. ABI is the Association of British Investigators, the professional regulatory body of British detectives. Its logo of a wavy flag inside a double circle is to detectives what checkatrade.com is to plumbers.]

AM:  Can you explain briefly what that case involved, so that readers can understand its relevance to my missing persons inquiry for 'I', aka 'Not-Mary', the author of these diaries?

Private detective Vince Johnson,
adviser on how not to discover the writer of anonymous diaries,
shortly before his escape from Libya, 2012.

VJ: It concerned a young man who, for identification purposes, I will call Jacob. He had escaped from a secure mental-health unit in Belgium and his parents believed that he might have come to Cambridge. It was not the first time he had gone walkabout. On the last occasion it took his family ten months to track him down to a park bench in Lyons, France. He was in a bedraggled state, virtually a 'vegetable' and unable to communicate. It was a sad case, about trying to save a disturbed young man's life.

AM: I believe you were praised for your 'unrelenting and tenacious' pursuit.

VJ: Interpol told the father that there had been a withdrawal of cash at one of the Market Street cash-points. The family sent me three photographs. He looked like every other young man in Cambridge. Like your Not-Mary, he did not have any friends, did not use his mobile, was very unsociable, used cash so as to be untraceable and had an intellect bordering on genius.

AM: At least you had a name.

VJ: He was a ghost.

How do you find a ghost? 'It goes without saying,' wrote Vince in his summary of the case, 'that I systematically searched the city by car, bicycle and on foot.' He became 'totally immersed'.

'I was of the view that I was the only person that was in full control of everything that was happening, and other people didn't understand and I would get angry and frustrated.'

VJ:     When I had rests I would speak with old police colleagues and serving members of the forces. I even sat down with my old pal George the Greek and asked the view of the man on the street. I wanted to be sure that I was covering every angle. The guy was deteriorating. It was like, 'Christ, you've got X amount of days to save this guy's life, because deterioration starts as soon as he stops taking his medication.' I did my best to climb inside his head and began acting like him. My wife is pretty good about things, but I was driving round and round and I thought, 'Goodness, what's that smell?' I hadn't had a shower for three or four days, and I was smelling like him. Jacob was certainly no mug. He had refined his technique after each escape, leaving virtually no footprints and becoming the invisible man.

AM:     But you still found him within two weeks in a city of 120,000 people?

VJ:     Sometimes you have to become obsessed to get it sorted out, and I suppose I do have an obsessive streak.

AM:     What was your breakthrough?

VJ:     A book, as with your diarist. It was a book of astronomy.


It is such a pleasure to see a lot come out of a little. For a moment I felt we were united: me and Not-Mary and Vince and Jacob, all taking delight in finding something large hidden inside something small. For Vince, not even knowing the book title, just knowing what it was about, gave him the solution to the most complex investigation of his career (he calls the case 'the great white shark in a pool of goldfish'). For me, in the minuscule handwriting of an anonymous, ill-tempered, dead old woman, I think, despite all my attempts to mock myself for being pompous and grandiose, that I have found something universal – a common mood that has not been explored before. For Not-Mary, 'pleasure' is the wrong word, but she is beset by the resonance of tiny things (her fear of being choked by particles of food; her huge ambition squashed into tiny letters; her hopes compared to 'the sprinkled oats' in the farmland next to Whitefield). For mad Jacob, out of equations on a page, the universe.

AM:   I don't understand. How was the book important?
VJ    I rang Jacob's mother and asked what was the last thing her son had been reading before he escaped from the asylum. She said it was about astronomy.
AM:   And why did that help?
VJ:   I went to the department of astronomy.
AM:   And?
VJ:   Waited.

After several days, Jacob showed up at the faculty. He was emaciated, 'bedraggled' and 'close to death'. There followed chases, secret videoing, calls to Belgian psychiatrists, international cooperation between Cambridge and European police forces, a stint for Jacob in the city mental hospital, and finally, with Vince sitting alongside Jacob in the back of an ambulance, entertaining him with a photograph album showing Jacob's favourite holiday places, a drive back to the asylum in Belgium.

It wasn't just his tenacity that won Vince his award, it was his psychological insight and his kindness.

In the same year that Vince cracked this complex missing persons case, he made local headlines by escaping across the desert from Libya at the start of the civil war against Colonel Gaddafi.

A week before our meeting I had sent Vince a selection of photocopies from Not-Mary's diaries. One included the following entry, made in 1974, when Not-Mary was thirty-five:

Still loving Dame Harriette extremely – wish I could love her less. Seem to have such a crush on her, I feel quite ashamed of myself. And it affects me physically most. My anguish would be awful if I lost her in any way, in fact. Of course worry about my health and ability to cope, in view of being in charge of something so precious. My little love, my little jewel, my little flower. She is 99.

'I did a bit of preliminary research for you before I came out this morning,' said Vince, extracting some photocopies from a stockbroker's briefcase that he'd been keeping hidden beside his chair legs. The top sheet, which he quickly turned over, was a photograph of me. Next, something that looked a little like a bank statement – he turned that over hurriedly too – then picked out the extract about Not-Mary's 'crush' on Dame Harriette, above.

VJ:    This person, 'Dame Harriette' (*tapping the name*).

AM:    I don't know who that is.

VJ:    She's a chick.

AM:    Not-Mary clearly thinks so.

VJ:    Her name is Chick. Dame Harriette Chick. One of seven sisters. Born in 1875, died 1977. A leading nutritionist. Her papers are in the Wellcome Library in London.

Dame Harriette Chick and her six sisters. Harriette is at the centre, in the white hat. She went on to become one of the leading microbiologists of her time, instrumental in finding a cure for rickets. Portrait photographs in her early career show a pugnacious young woman wearing a collar and tie, with frizzy hair gathered at the sides in flat bunches, about the size of oven mitts. Her attractive, strong head looks like someone taking a loaf of bread out of the range.

VJ:     Does this reference back to the severed pages you
        mention?
AM:     How would that be possible? That book was written in
        1952, when Not-Mary was thirteen. The entry about
        Dame Harriette is a quarter of a century later.
VJ:     (*Tilting his head as if no combination of events is too
        peculiar for this world.*) Perhaps she uses an old book.
        Hides her thoughts there? Now she wants to eradicate
        that particular part of her life. I've had cases like that.
        She wouldn't want her diaries contaminated by this
        person. A lot of people, to save their sanity, will take
        out every reference to that person. Take it out of your
        life, then it won't hurt you. I can't imagine any other
        reason why a person wants to cut out huge pieces of
        text when, at that stage, she still has aspirations of
        being published.

Vince picked up another photocopy I'd sent him, and
compared the early large handwriting with the late cramped
script. 'Did you buy a finite number of books, all at the start?'
he asked, addressing not me, but Not-Mary. For the next
few minutes as he studied the pages he muddled his tenses
and subjects as though he were testing combinations on a
safe to find a way in – sometimes he spoke *as* Not-Mary;
sometimes to her; sometimes he addressed, a little coldly,
me or himself. 'Maybe she knew something about herself.
It seems strange to start writing in one size and then going
to a size that is about half. She is running out of space, time,
the end is coming.

Only a certain amount of time left, then she will try and
get everything in those exercise books and hence write small.
There isn't any tremor in this writing. It's very precise . . .

punctuation better than in the earlier books . . . almost too small. Why is it too small? She's obviously got very good eyesight. Yes . . . she acknowledges to herself that she isn't going to get published and so why bother? Why make it legible? No, make it as small as my own private life. In the end, the diaries are the only place she has left . . .'

I was interested in Vince's psychological metaphors of enclosure and location. 'I's diary is the emblem of her oppressive life, her handwriting the measure of her sense of unimportance; as she writes in her pages, so she sits, diminished, a frightened and lonely middle-aged woman in her room. When Vince was chasing Jacob, he interpreted the man's behaviour in a similar way. It turned out there was a good reason why Vince hadn't been able to find Jacob on the streets or in any of the hostels or hotels around the city. After spotting him in the astronomy department, he followed him secretly, 'dodging behind trees to keep up'.

VJ:     I was obviously expecting Jacob to lead me to a guest house or student digs, and was quite excited because I had him in my sights and it was dark. He walked to where I had parked my car and – I wasn't expecting this at all – he jumped into a bloody hire car. I had to dive over the bonnet out of sight and into my car. I had to drive over a grassy bank, smack down on the other side, to follow him. He came to a stop in Storey's Way, got out, took his laptop out of the back, then got back into the car and started studying. The car was his classroom. His face was illuminated by the glow of his laptop. Then he got into a sleeping bag and the car was his hotel. In his mind, the car was these different rooms.

During the time Vince was telling me about Jacob he had been glancing through the photocopies I'd sent him of the severed notebook, and was now studying the drawing of the psychotic woman (see p.100).

VJ:     There's something wrong here. The eyes of the baby: it looks like an alien. That baby is not human-looking. It's almost like the mother is cross. Why is the mother angry? The mouth is like these modern-day dollybirds with the pouting look. It doesn't go with the cross expression. No, that is not a pleasant face . . . I love my mother, but because Mum is angry with me, I have got to have relationships with older women? When she refers to her health in that note about Dame Harriette, maybe she's referring to her mental health. You are looking at a woman in her mid-thirties, perhaps mentally unwell and has a crush on her employer who is ninety-nine who died three years later . . . How did she die? Maybe we do have a crime?

AM:     I don't think she was crazy like that. Not enough to be locked up in an asylum like Jacob. She was lonely, disappointed, not mad.

VJ:     She was locked up in her own asylum.

That was enough. I didn't want to give Vince any more. I didn't want him to win another award for solving this mystery too. My initial reason for contacting him was not because I wanted to know what techniques to use to track down my missing diarist, but the opposite. I wanted to know how to avoid the successful approaches.

Vince explained that the first thing I needed to do was look up the electoral register. I determined never to go near the thing.

VJ:     What happens if she wasn't murdered and she's not a spy or a brilliant scientist and there's no big secret; there's nothing significant about her – she's just an ordinary person?

AM:     But that's exactly the point. That's the best result. As long as Not-Mary remains unknown, she's valuable. Her ordinariness, and the fact that she has written so much about it, is what makes her interesting. If she was famous, that would ruin it. If she was a scandal, or a politician or a pop star, she will stop being the faceless person next door. I'm in trouble then.

Vince got up to go. He clipped open his surprising briefcase and returned into it my photocopies and the background documentation about me.

'You know, with 148 diaries, your trouble is going to be not enough troubles.'

Then he swung his branch around his trunk again and shook my hand goodbye.

# 17  The Second stabbing

> Crumbs, however am I going to get through life like this?
> *Sat, April 2nd, 1960*

> Luckily, not too afraid of Blue Danish cheese
> *Wed, March 30th, 1960*
> **Aged twenty**

On April 3rd, 1960, Not-Mary began stabbing walls.

She'd spent the morning in 'utter mooching and idleness, obstinate in my depression'. Her sisters had 'irritated around'. At lunch, 'too angry & worked up' to eat, she sat at the dining table with her hands on either side of her empty plate 'jumping like fishes'. She winced at her family's juicy gluttony.

Not-Mary had been struck by a horrific idea: what happens if, when I swallow, the food goes into my lungs by accident? After a few months, what had started as a small mental tic – one of dozens of such things that plague children every day, and which most of us manage quickly to sweep aside – had in Not-Mary's case become a full-blown neurosis, which Not-Mary called 'The Phobia'. I had one of these too. Mine started aged seven when my American parents took me back to the US. Driving down a freeway one morning we passed a restaurant called 'The Stop and Stuff Inn'. For some reason – who knows why? – that phrase fixed in my head and pounded there for two years: *Stop and Stuff Inn, Stop and Stuff Inn, Stop and Stuff Inn, Stop and Stuff Inn* . . . Even now, four decades later, I feel nervous putting the words down. I used to wake up in the night feeling like vomiting because I couldn't get rid of them.

For Not-Mary, the horror of solid food quickly spread to gulps of drink (sips, even at The Phobia's worst, she could always manage). At mealtimes it took her up to two hours of nibbling to finish a single plate. The canteens at her sixth-form college, and then later at art school, were impossible. She could not make friends or go out with men. Even Lyon's Corner Houses were troublesome: always there was a piece of cake. Dehydrated and in despair, she developed cystitis, so The Phobia spread to toilets. If she wasn't jittery because she was about to eat, she was panicking because she couldn't pee.

One of the things I like about Not-Mary is that these early troubles have such a strong physical representation. Memoirs so often split their bindings with whining explanations of psychological traumas – Daddy didn't love me; Mummy slapped me when I was four. Not-Mary never blames her parents for this madness of hers. It's nothing to do with parents. There is a time when she goes to see a psychiatrist and he comes out with the expected erotic guff, particularly excited by the word 'swallowing'; but his observations don't have much effect on Not-Mary. Not-Mary's difficulties came down to the beginning and end of her digestive tract. The beginning: the result of a childish mental tic about eating that might happen to anybody, but that had, in her case, got out of hand. The end: cystitis. On top of this are the understandable consequences of being reminded every month that you bleed, that your function is to produce babies, like a farm animal, and that no matter how much you plead for the help and support of your body during A-Level exam week, your innards will always be willing to betray you and start spasmodic cramping.

Ever since my visit to the petrol station, I've thought it a wonder that any woman is sane.

*

If Not-Mary could just have sorted out the processes of ingestion and excrement, her life in the early 1960s might have been all right.

She started to lose weight. On March 17th, 1960, she was 10 stone 2 pounds; on May 7th, 9 stone 13½.

> Watch with hysterical dread my increasing slimness, with horror at the thought of becoming a "walking skeleton".

Her fear was not translated back into lack of appetite. She'd have gnawed lichen off the rocks if her oesophagus would have let her. But each time Not-Mary raised a fork to her mouth her throat seized up – snap! – and she could not get the food down.

The Phobia bounds after her across every page of these early diaries. In a dream Not-Mary imagined she was a cow, eating the grass: the earth was layered with food. But when she woke, another quarter of a pound had gone.

> It's uncomfortable now to sit on a hard stool, my bones coming through.

She devised elaborate tricks to try to get nutrients in. Lying on her back on the bed, she dangled her head over the edge and tried to eat upside down. That way (with gravity on her side) she had more control over which route the food took when it reached the vital divide between lungs and stomach. She hid behind the family car and pushed a bun into her mouth 'directly from a paper bag' without letting her eyes see what she was up to. It didn't work. Another method was to lock herself in the bathroom, put her head in the basin, turn on the tap, and eat to the sound of running water. There was no rationale to this last one as far as I could make out. It succeeded now and then.

'To write,' she notes during one twenty-page entry, 'creates a drive to live; "swallowing" a drive to die.'

On the day of stabbing that opened this chapter, Not-Mary's 'repulsive' young sisters had hurriedly started putting on their coats after their gluttonous lunch, because they'd wanted to visit Granny for supper, and start guzzling all over again.

Appalled, Not-Mary had quietly stood up from the table and said she didn't want to join them. She'd said she might go to Bedford instead, and watch *Madam Butterfly* at the cinema.

Then she'd said she felt a bit tired for Bedford.

She would just go to bed.

After that, she'd walked upstairs to her room and attacked the wallpaper with a penknife.


The Phobia, like the curse, was rarely absent, but was never at its worst for more than a week. The rest of the time it lingered behind Not-Mary's chair during meals like a not very good butler, part of a cluster of smaller mental upsets that made her life miserable.

There was also the fear she had about crossing roads, and the nervousness about riding bicycles; the conviction that she smelled, was stupid, was doomed to spinsterhood, was hated; the suspicion that she was about to lose her arms and her sight because what she wanted more than anything was to be a writer or painter or musician, and it would be just like God to take away the two bits of her needed for these things; the intermittent agoraphobia . . .

The oppressive butler behind Not-Mary's chair was not a man; it was an octopus.

There's lots of room here for psychobabble. But I'm still not especially worried for Not-Mary. Her clang-bang view of herself is more than the usual adolescent mental cacophony, maybe, but kids get through this. They sort it out. At twenty-one, Not-Mary's also a little old for such nonsense, but she's grown up in a wood on top of a four-million-year-old hill.

At the back of the stabbing diary, where the top edge has eroded into the shape of limestone cliffs, she fantasises about pain and killing:

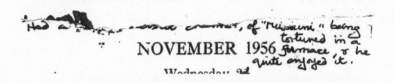

Had a dream . . . of "Mussolini" being
tortured in a
furnace, & he
quite enjoyed it.
*(Actual date May 1960)*

Wond[er if] I am a potential murderer – my feelings
become so p[oi]senous – don't even feel blind rage – just a
desire for pure revenge for my woes, a bitter cruelty.
Am a potential suicide anyway

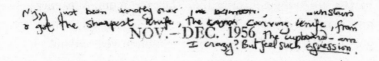

## NOV. – DEC. 1956

Nizzy [her mother] just been beastly over the bedroom, ... downstairs
& got the sharpest knife, the carving knife, from
the cupboard – am
I crazy? But feel such <u>agression</u>.

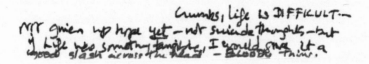

Crumbs, life is DIFFICULT –
Not given up hope <u>yet</u> – not suicide thoughts – but
if Life was something tangible, I would give it a
good slash across the head – BLOODY thing.

Soon after she left the Perse School for Girls, Not-Mary, still
only nineteen, began work on her 'third novel' ('it is not
quite as good as Dr Zhivago'). She had ambitions also to be
'an authority & writer on Shakespeare'.

Want to write as well as novels, plays, opera, & songs
... lovely spring weather – winds, blown from
heaven, fitful sun, rain, the trees roaring, whipped me
up to a frenzy of excitement.

Her artistry raged not just for literature, but also for music and painting:

> I am an individual, born to create, not to go with the masses! Look at my reflection – a profound sort of young face – in the mirror of the 'bus window, and think that I am not a librarian, or a cook . . . not even a student of English at the university, a scholar – but an artist, (but after being an artist in several mediums, would be a scholar).

In a biography of Thomas Mann, she'd read that the true artist is 'isolated & different, rejected by his fellow normal human beings'. Goethe, according to the book, was a well-known social fruitcake.

> I may – perhaps – have colossal powers in me.

It was in order to be closer to the 'the quiet, clock-ticking library temperament' that she took a room near the centre of Cambridge, next door to where her maternal grandparents lived, on Castle Hill.

> Wonderful, gorgeous lodgings . . . Lovely view out of bedroom window – Kings College, & a panorama of Cambridge rooves, churches, & spires – smoking chimneys & blue slate tiles & tossing trees & dramatic skies.

The Cambridge house where Not-Mary had her lodgings during this period is about a quarter of a mile from where Dido would find the diaries in the skip forty-four years later. Not-Mary's landlady was Miss Ramsey, the aunt of Michael

Ramsey, the Archbishop of Canterbury.

Miss Ramsey charged twenty-five shillings a week, bills and breakfast included, and Not-Mary had to move out of the room whenever the godly nephew dropped by.

> The 'Archbish' has slept in my bed the last two nights – he came into the Reading Room today – little did he know he spoke to the girl whose bed he'd slept in last night.

On such occasions, Not-Mary stayed with her grandparents next door. She rarely mentions these relatives, though she must have seen a great deal of them during this period. But she mentions looking in one of their mirrors.

> Saw in the glass in Granny's room, my own face – it has changed again – still a bit small and thin, but well-looking & above all, it has more soul – which must be the radiance Mrs W. spoke of. The clear brow, the intense large eyes behind the light spectacles, the delicate half-smiling mouth & artist's chin.

As soon as Archbishop Ramsey returned to Canterbury Miss Ramsey would puff up the pillows, replace the sheets and let Not-Mary back in.

'This fugitive bliss of Miss Ramsey's I adore,' wrote Not-Mary in a small red memo book.

> The "Archbish" has been using my <u>pink soap</u>.

These eyes are intense and large; the mouth is delicate and half smiling.
But she still looks like a boxer in a wig, now with make-up. I don't know
what an 'artist's' chin is.

I've got it wrong about Whiters again. Another biographical fact
I thought I had fixed has gone *poooooffff!* and disappeared.

Whitefield wasn't her family home. Not-Mary hadn't been
born there. It was a place about which she fantasised. The only
time Not-Mary stayed at Whitefield, which was owned by her
paternal grandmother, was when she was a pupil at the Perse
Girls, between the ages of sixteen and eighteen.

Not-Mary was born thirty miles away, in a house in Haynes,
outside Bedford, where

> All the buildings squat & ugly & dirty, and the people
> looking both stupid & repulsive . . .

As usual with Not-Mary's style of writing, it's difficult to build
up a solid picture of what the Haynes house was like. It had the
vulgar name of 'Tudor Cottage'. It was close to a main road. I
imagine a house on a terrace corner with a low garden wall that
faces into a crossroads; white textured walls; a wood-stained
1930s portico stuck between two bay windows containing
pieces of bottle glass; asthmatic rosebushes with car soot under
the leaves. The more I think about it, the more I dirty up the
walls and ruin the flowerbeds. Haynes, during these post-war
years, was kept awake by lorries transporting seething cargoes
of fresh-baked building stock from the brickworks at Stewartby
to supply the housing boom in the east.

Not-Mary mentions the difficulty of getting to sleep.

Living with her in Tudor Cottage were her mother, two of her
sisters ('the sharp-tongued and naggy Woill, and that large-
faced, smelly brat which is my sister Kate') and her father, 'a
stingy stick' who is mentioned as little as possible. In one of the
diaries there's a sketch of the house that also mentions a
character called Bendlow, who might be a servant or the toilet:

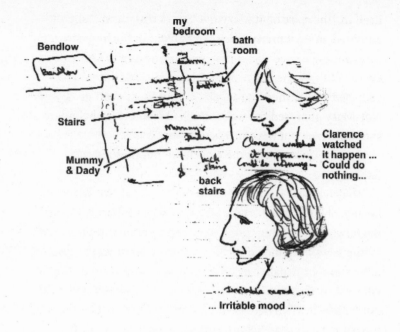

When her mother reached the top of the stairs during the wall-stabbing episode, Not-Mary, still holding the penknife, cried out, 'I won't come with you in the car to visit Whiters since you'd be ashamed of me; but I'll probably cut my wrists whilst everyone is away.'

They forced her to come to Whiters.

During the thirty-mile drive Not-Mary huddled in the back of the car. The strength of her emotions had terrified her. The journey passed through ugly towns followed by slow, over-farmed hills. Much of the way was a blur of hedgerows. None of it had the brilliant, almost painful sense of experience that true life ought to have for an artist. It zipped noiselessly by.

Only when the car reached the village of Great Shelford, close to Whiters, did the hollowness of her mood start to fill itself in. The spire of St Mary the Virgin church was, she admitted, at least pretty. The land in front of the high street pub – Saxons once lived there; that was comforting to know. At every field gate the hedges running alongside Hinton Way vanished and flashed back again, and in those swift gaps Not-Mary glimpsed the wooded sea of Cambridge below; she could pick out the conceited college spires.

Her sister Kate was at the wheel, not her mother or father.

'To drive a car is coming on in life,' declared Not-Mary to herself. She was awed by the way Kate veered sharply through the howl of oncoming traffic, shot between the gateposts into Whitefield's tree-lined drive and, quickly adjusting the gear lever and foot pedals, eased past the 'pink-coppery rustling wheat with the poppies growing in between'. Not-Mary could not believe it when her sister later said that, in that deft blur of movements, she had 'felt no nervousness'.

Kate 'is turning out in life much better than me'.

On this evening after the wall-stabbing episode, Not-Mary asked to be let out at the bottom of the drive so she could walk up along the avenue of lime trees alone. She needed that, she explained, to give her time to return to herself. Only at Whitefield House, whether she was living there or not, did Not-Mary feel she had a real identity. Only at Whitefield was she not Not-Mary, the outcast, the woman who will go to her death nameless and be thrown out in a skip, but

'Laura!' cried her grandmother, flinging open the front door. 'Welcome!'

# 18  Growing up

I am too tall.

**Aged thirty-five**

On the train back from meeting Vince, I had had a shocking idea. I realised I could bring 'I' back from the grave and measure her height.

'I' mentions that she is tall. Her size bent over her. Disgusted by it, she had a stoop and walked oddly.

> E said I am nothing but a tall child.

> E said I walk like some one who is not quite right.

> E said Mrs Sophia looks after a girl who walks like I do, and she gets hysterical and right out of her mind.

> E said Laura you are . . .

That's how I'd discovered the diarist's name was Laura: by reading it in one of E's dehumanising attacks while I was searching for clues about the diarist's height.

Now I realised I didn't need to wait for Laura to tell me the answer; I could calculate it. I stared through the train window at the passing countryside with remembered triumph – Laura! Her name was Laura! – and sensed that everything was a symbol. The woodland running along one side of the railway tracks was my ignorance. The view on the other side across sunlit irrigation streams to a village church – that was the revelation of 'I's Christian name. The sudden blocking of this view by a B&Q warehouse with garish orange signage represented my professionalism: although pleased to have uncovered this name, I was not going to let myself be distracted by it. A name is just a name. One must not draw cheap and superficial conclusions. All the same, I had never been able to picture Not-Mary as tall. Not-Mary is a short person's name. 'Laura' has stature.

It's important to know what this height is, because Laura's attitude to it is peculiar. In middle age she refused to shop in Budgens because of the way she teetered over the 'short people' who went to that store so that they looked at her and spotted that she was buying cider. But how tall exactly was she? She never specifies. Was she a giantess?

The average height of a British woman in the 1950s, when Laura left the Perse Girls, was five feet two inches. Today it is five feet four inches. (According to an article in the *Daily Mail*, this is partly due to central heating: because we spend less energy shivering as we grow up, we put more energy into growing taller.) But this is still shrimpish. The women I know who are five foot nine don't talk about their height. If Laura is only that tall, then we learn something about her state of mind – she is suffering from paranoia. At five foot ten, women start to mention it. After six feet some get a worried look at the top of their nose. The tallest woman I know is six foot two – she has a stoop. Was that Laura's height?

At my train stop I hurried to the stationer's, and exited minutes later with a small piece of plastic that had cost me 45p. With this item I could take Laura out of her grave and uncurl her as certainly as if she'd been laid in front of me. I had ferreted out her sex, exposed her date of birth, stumbled on her Christian name – now I was going to calculate her measurements. Her fogginess was being blown away.

The solution to the question of her height is in the colourful books from the late 1990s, when she is old. It is on every page. For example, here:

I let Peter imprison me every summer evening in the usual way – abysmal, when others are out and about.

And here:

Peter came upstairs as usual, to make his bed and all that; but changed his mind, had to hurry down to the wickery. He eats so much tinned grapefruit etc. etc.. I just wanted revenge for all the misery he has caused me – turned on the hot taps everywhere I could, so that he would lose all his hot water. I knew he would sit helpless in the wickery, whilst it all ran away. And then he would not be able to flush the pee out of his basin.

The key is the slope of the script. These books were written at night while Laura was lying on her bed, so the tilt of the line represents the curve made as her hand moves across the page, while her elbow (acting as pivot) remains resting on the mattress. In other words, it should be possible to use the angle and length of this downward gradient to estimate the length of the writer's forearm. (If she were a dwarf, her forearm would be correspondingly small, and the sentences bent to a ridiculous degree; if a giant, hardly any curvature at all.) The 45p plastic object I needed to resurrect Laura from the dead was the same thing Barbara had used to study her handwriting: a school protractor.

I worked at my equations through the night. By dawn I had the answer.

Let S be the average length of a line of a late diary entry.

Let A be the average angle made by this line of text to the horizontal.

If S be taken to represent the secant of a circle with radius 'length of Laura's forearm plus the distance from there to the writing tip of her pen', Laura's height will be given by

$$6 \times 0.68 \times S \div (2 \times \sin A)$$

The factor 0.68 comes from experiments (conducted on myself) which have found that the length of a person's forearm is 0.68 times the distance from his or her elbow to the point of the pen:

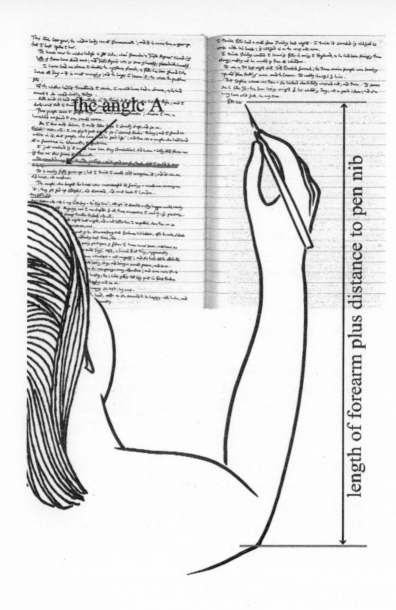

the angle A

length of forearm plus distance to pen nib

The factor 6 is due to the well-established empirical fact, as described on the internet, that a person's height is roughly six times the length of their forearm.

Ergo, putting into the equation the length and angle of Laura's later diary lines:

$$\text{Laura uncurled} = 6 \times 0.68 \times [S \div (2 \times \sin A)]$$
$$= 6 \times 0.68 \times [0.13 \div 0.0698]$$
$$= 7.6$$

Seven metres, sixty centimetres, or just under twenty-five feet tall.

I snatched up my page and threw it in the fire.

# 19 Sex

Laura: 'But was it sex?'

E (*'vehemently'*): 'Of course it was!'

**Aged twenty-three**

After the Perse School for Girls and the loss of her job at the public library, Laura stopped work on her Pasternakian novels and focused on painting. She went to Luton Modern School and Technical College to study art. The Modern School would eventually become the University of Bedford, but at this time it was still a vocational secondary school, and Laura's days were hard and busy. She forgot E in Cambridge, and fell so much in love with the etching master that she couldn't see his nose:

> How singular are Mr Stewart's artistic, temperamental & intellectual qualities. If E couldn't have my diaries should I <u>die</u>, he can have them.

> Such fervour, intellectualism and fire! How surprised my family would be if they knew I bequeathed these precious volumes to an almost total stranger! But it is a question of soul . . .

> Still don't know what his nose is like.

The night after her first class she slept, thrilled, 'an artist's sleep, a mere suspension of consciousness . . . What a jewel Mr Stewart is (is that his name, or is he Mr Mullin?)'

In the diaries from the sixties, Laura uses her private expression for 'erotic': 'c-feely'. E is 'c-feely'. The actor who played the Bishop in a production of *The Lark* by Jean Anouilh that she saw in Cambridge one August is 'c-feely'. John Gielgud is 'v c-feely'.

Various crude words suggest themselves for that 'c', but 'c-feely' isn't pornographic. Laura isn't being coy. If she wants to record that she's thinking about sex (which is quite often) she bursts out with ecstasy:

I am a sexy one!

'C-feely' means weeping, high-cheekboned, misunderstood men committing suicide in draughty rented accommodation. 'C-feely' is about penetration of the spirit, not the body. It's not cunt-feely or cock-feely; it's a word that suggests purity of soul.

Noseless Mr Stewart is c-feely. She hopes he is going to die of consumption. But even she can see that's a bit too Katherine Mansfield (one of her favourite writers), so she toughens up and calls it tuberculosis:

> Can see him getting T.B. – his face is already
> insubstantial, too ethereal, eyes too bright and
> feverish. Can see him well in the vast shadowy studio,
> & himself painting, lonely, hungry, emotional, fired
> by creating. Wonder if he is married – hope not.
> He very much genius in the attic, or a dying poet.

You don't have pornographic sex with a man whose face is disappearing. You 'sit on the sofa, leaning back against him with my head lying on his shoulder and perhaps just talk a little, occasionally, of deep things'.

With c-feely man, the emphasis is on emotional embrace and *safety* from popping trouser buttons. She lusts for a man who fails to suppress his lust, but his desire should be metaphorical (e.g. a wild enthusiasm for something artistic, a 'lust for life') or allegorical (e.g. migraine, consumption). She's not particular which; she just wants him isolated and then felled by longing. It must destroy his calm.

But that night after her class with Mr Stewart/Mullin, something went amiss. Laura dreamt of the wrong person: not of the one with the missing proboscis, but of Mr Finch, who teaches life-drawing – a very different box of pencils. Nothing about Mr Finch was insubstantial. He was 'very nicely set-up. A perfect man's body – essentially masculine'; 'lovely steady firm man's hands, bespeaking a steady mind'.

Laura's dream about Mr Finch was not 'c-feely'. It was 'strangely beautiful'.

The next morning, rather flushed, she spotted him in the canteen, smashing potatoes down onto his gammon and pineapple slice.

'No glamour in him,' she records muttering to herself as she hurried past to collect her beaker of water from the cistern. 'Very dull.'


A week later, Laura's lust came to a head. Again, her thoughts were on the noseless one; again, her loins went to Mr Finch. 'A marvellous day!' she gasped afterwards, crouched over her blue Collins 'Royal Diary', still trying to catch her breath. The card boards of this book are napped from excessive handling, which is why they have the texture of felt. 'Think I have discovered something about the mystery of sex – thrilling.'

Was doing life-drawing, Mr Finch came and sat close behind me – in fact, so close that his whole front was pressing up against my back as he stretched out his arm, drawing to explain what he said.

Then a curious thing happened – as that firm, kindly, steady man's body pressed against mine, a wonderful, tickling, tingling, deep pleasure made itself felt throughout my whole body – perhaps particularly in the region of my lower stomach, but everywhere else too. It had a slight element of discomfort in it, as if I were in fact, being tickled by someone or something inside my body – but it was wonderful before anything else, and a complete novelty in pure physical sensation.

It was a thrilling surprise – and is it sex?

'Is that feeling I had what the medical books call an "orgasm"?' she added later. She often sneaked into bookshops during this period to peek through textbooks, to get a sense of what life was up to. 'Although got no emission with it, if that is involved,' she noted after one such trip.

If this was sex, a little of its mystery is unravelled, and perhaps the idea of 'going to bed' with a man isn't as silly as I thought – not if it feels like that.

One might be tempted to think that the feeling was just imagination – but my experience of life makes me doubt that – for one thing, it was a strong and definite physical sensation . . . think this must be a universal part of human nature – the so-far not-understood, **carnal-desire**.

Laura is not rash, however. She knows she must be careful not to get carried away with this leaning business. 'Step by step,' she writes (and the sentence can be read in almost any tone from prissiness to bored harlotry), 'one gets more & more deeply involved, without noticing it – thus I suppose illegitimate babies are born.'

The odd part is, though she thinks Mr Finch is 'beautiful', she does not find him attractive. It is his man-ness that rouses her. This makes her reflect on another 'curious thing': 'how does my body know that it is a <u>man</u> leaning against me, without any mental excitement about him involved – why does one get that feeling with a man, and not, for instance, with the back of a bus seat?'

After **carnal-desire** there is an unusual three-quarter-inch gap of no writing on the page of the diary. Perhaps it signifies a pause in her thoughts. Perhaps it is a joyous leap.

'Wanted,' begins the next sentence, 'no more than for Mr Finch to <u>go on</u> leaning against me . . .'


Laura *had* got the lovely Mr Stewart's name wrong. He wasn't called Mr Mullin either: his name was J. Sturgess. And she never, in the two years she flirted with him at Luton, discovered what that J stood for. He was 'J. Sturgess' according to the timetable in the hall; he was 'J. Sturgess' when she lingered, whistling, in the corridor for the coast to clear, then shot into the staff room to check the tutors' board; he was 'J. Sturgess' on the name tag that could just be (if you crouched down) picked out in the shaft of light slipping through the gap at the top of his locked desk drawer. What did that fish-hook letter refer to? James? Jeffrey? Junior? She never asked.

With all his missing attributes, it's occurred to me that J. Sturgess didn't exist. But it's not true. He's real. Last week I received an email from him. He's alive, still a painter, replies only through his wife's account, and wants nothing to do with me.

> I was only at Luton for a short while and cannot
> remember the students. I am sorry I can't help you.

Each week on Tuesday Mr Sturgess appeared on his motorbike at Luton College at 5.30 p.m., stayed for precisely sixty minutes, then hurried away 'as if it has all been a bit much for him'.

Laura brought a couple of 'Attention-Seeking-Devices' to trap him. One was a reproduction of Lotte Reiniger paper silhouettes of *Swan Lake*.

She asked Mr Sturgess's opinion about these impish coils as soon as possible, 'so I could look at his wonderful eyes,

and hear him talk, & be nice to me. He <u>did</u> talk.'

He declared the cut-outs 'not art'.

Laura was charmed. Joining forces with a bunch of the teddy boys in the class, she got him stoked up about what *was* art:

> He talked of what E spoke of, reaching after something one can't get – he described it as 'agony'. His temperament is wonderfully excitable – gets very worked up – a slight remark can make him 'blow up', wax mighty hot & passionate! What fire! He is marvellous. Can see him in my mind's eye, weeping in his studio because he can't get what he seeks – the 'agony' he spoke of.

Laura began to 'forget myself, pour out my deeper thoughts. I am the most intellectual and cultured student in the class . . .'

'Some of the things he said, I was rather out of my depth,' she admits defiantly, but 'I understood him better than the others – they asked such stupid questions – & when they all came up to listen, breathing heavily and open-mouthed, the magic circle was broken & came back to earth with a bump – "'Ow much d'yer get fer yer pintins, Sir?" '

By the end of her year at Luton, life was peachy. Laura had won a place at Camberwell School of Art to study illustration. She and Sturgess had become friends. On her last day at the college she put on her favourite striped suit for him and they walked out of the class together to say goodbye in the car park.

Luton Technical College, at the time Laura was a student.
'Of the "Toppled Cornflake Boxes School" of school design,'
writes Dr Jonathan Foyle, formerly of the World Monuments Fund.
(© The Francis Frith Collection)

'Be careful on your bike, gifted people have more to lose,' she shouted as Sturgess throttled up, his face 'rather young and thin under the helmet'. 'If you ever want a free lunch, come to visit me in London!'

'I'll avail myself much of the opportunity,' he shouted back, noselessly.

Sturgess was twenty-seven years old, had been married for two years, was vegetarian ('my tastes are so in common with his, it is wonderful'), and sped off 'as a sealed package at the registrar's office'.

## 20  What a queer set up

> Felt particularly bitter against the college
> today. They have given me only 42 for my
> fairground comp. And 43 for life.
>
> **Aged  twenty-two**

'Mr Ellis

at me.

I am physically afraid of the man, he is so

big

& so

coarse

& so violent .

1961, July 14th. Hardback pocketbook, parcel-paper binding. Glue rotted. Text with numerous signs of distress: crossings-out, inability to stick to the line, erratic letters. The sentences on the final page suddenly small and backed up, suggesting Laura hadn't noticed the end of the book approaching so rapidly, scrabbled desperately to avoid hitting it, staved off disaster by snatching up stray sheets of paper from around her desk until finally the dreadful story is finished, and she is forced to make the leap into the next book. Seven folded inserts are stuffed inside the back cover.

This diary begins brightly. The opening page is Laura's last day at Luton Art College. A week later she sets off for Liverpool. She'd landed a two-month summer post as a housekeeper/cook with a family in the Wirral: light cleaning, two meals a day. The advert had appeared in *The Lady*.

But from the start there was something unsettling about the arrangement. Even the journey up, through the Pennines, felt oppressive: 'breathtaking scenery, such colossal heights', such 'depths – great cliff-like hills and wooded steeps'; the train sucked her into tunnels, snorted her along under mountains, spat her into new valleys; the world outside 'overpowered me, gave me claustrophobia', the sky 'filled with dazzling white light, the sun in its zenith'.

At Liverpool station she was met, not by her supposed employer, Mr Ellis, but by a mysterious 'girl model', a 'beautiful & very nice, not made-up' Spaniard. The young woman appeared not to speak English, and drove her silently through the Mersey Tunnel ('marvellous feat of engineering – well relieved to get out of it'). Laura could not find out why the previous employee had left unexpectedly and suddenly. It was not unreasonable that Mr Ellis had chosen her from other potential candidates, because Laura had done housework jobs before and had references from previous employers. But weren't there any local girls who wanted work? Why pick someone who lived 160 miles away?

The 'girl model' continued driving silently.

Were adverts in *The Lady* always safe?

Laura describes the house as 'surrounded by vast empty open stretches of sands' that slope away towards a 'thin blue blade'. At high tide the sea comes right up to the walls, so that it appears to Laura that the house 'floats on the water'. It is, she writes, 'ghostly with wind'.

Mr Ellis turns out to be 'rather a "small" person, & rather conceited & complacent'. He has a 'man's lack of graciousness'. His wife, 'an oddish woman', claims to be a fashion designer and a painter; to Laura's astonishment she does not immediately try to befriend Laura. 'Her lack of feeling & interest for a fellow artist incredible.'

At my daughter's christening two years ago, an ex-school-teacher of mine, John Rogers (a theologian and author of *The Basic Bible*), gave an address in which he argued that the solution to the Trinity was that it was not a trinity at all, but a two-and-a-halfity. The Father and the Son are nouns, explained John, stepping away from the lectern and coming down the aisle in his enthusiasm about this point, but the Holy Spirit is a verb; it is 'the act of intercourse' between Father and Son.

Fresh from J. Sturgess, 'leaning' drawing masters and the discovery of sex, Laura in this 1961 book believes in Art in the same spirit: it is the 'act of intercourse' between the artist and the Essence.

Surely two people with the same glow of artistic ecstasy on their cheeks should recognise each other? thinks Laura as she walks upstairs behind Mrs Ellis to be shown her bedroom. She wonders if Mrs Ellis is a fake, 'a bit on the common side', and not a designer at all.

'Well, I am in a queer set up!' she writes that night, wallowing in pillows. The room she has been given has a window seat looking out across the sands to a moon-speckled sea; the furniture has been arranged with 'all sorts of furbelows, yet nowhere to put anything, not even my flannel'. Although this is supposed to be a temporary, low-paid, semi-skilled housekeeping job, she has been put in a four-poster bed.

### Sunday, June 25th
First whole day here – what a curious post, I don't have to do any work – so far, just a sort of guest. Got to sleep late last night – was so hungry visited the larder, & even that did not stop the pangs. It was the same this morning, ate what I could lay hands on.

### Monday, June 26th
Love having this lovely big comfy four poster. Love it when the sea reclaims the vast miles of sand, as it does this evening – the running tide almost up to the windows, as it were, vast watery wastes with the racing little breakers all round. Around sunset, a greenish clarity of sky; beamy radiance on the sea from stormy clouds. Little pools by the rocks with shimmery shells, wind-blown ruffled clear water.

### Thursday, June 29th
An extraordinarily happy day but love it here, everything is extremely nice . . . Wonderful to feel an unshadowed happiness, no tragedy; everything this summer is going all right for me; no mental conflict this summer, which is unusual for me. I enjoy my youth & health & gifts, and smile upon a smiling world.

**Friday, June 30th**

Still can't quite make out the Ellises.


**Saturday, July 1st**

A really busy day; this post isn't as simple as I thought, so many things to remember. The Bendix quite beyond me, & not very good in the laundry line. Unskilled at ironing. Mrs Ellis paid me £7 this morning (£2 was for my fare). That is a very nice little sum!


**Sunday, July 2nd**

A lot to do today. Hope the Ellises are satisfied with me. Took a ballet book on beach in afternoon – rich, sensitive enjoyment. The sea was lively & sparkly & exciting; a very windy day, rather cold. And in eve, the sea right out of sight, the vast distance of the sands, amazing, with other-planet, lunar aspect, grey, with bars, & craters of water.


**Monday, July 3rd**

Feeling extraordinarily happy, as happy as if I were in love. Wonder why I feel quite so happy, it isn't comfortable to feel it to such a degree.

Am reluctant to be evicted from my four-poster, & it hasn't happened yet, though Mrs. Ellis hinted today, but she is tolerant, I had already slept two nights overdue in their guest room.

**Tuesday, July 4th**

Mr. Ellis isn't very nice, always sees what I <u>don't</u> do, not what I <u>do</u> do . . .

**Wednesday, July 5th**

Have made a particularly funny & serious mistake here – given breast of lamb to the dog! Thought it was a scraggy old bit, & not good enough for the casserole. In spite of my discomfort at the revelation found it very funny, such a good story to tell.

Rather on the tired side, so not taking the work unduly quickly. Fagged away at laundry – it would have been better to have put it in the washing-machine.

Not yet been evicted from my four-poster!

**Sunday, July 9th**

Had a tummy-upset in the night – windy, spasmodic pains; wonder if being in labour feels rather like that. It must have been the lettuce, or over-eating generally.

The Ellises returned while I was out on my evening walk. Find them really very irritating. Mr. Ellis accused me of finishing up the bacon; I don't know what's happened to the blasted stuff. Could hear Mr. Ellis telling Mrs. Ellis . . .

### Tuesday, July 11th

Got a very nasty shock today – the Ellises have given me the sack. I have taken it tragically, feel it very much. Never dreamt I'd be sacked even on a <u>temporary</u> post. must have been very bad work; yet surely it couldn't have been, & I personally enjoyed the food I cooked.

### Wednesday, July 12th

What on earth is a person who cannot keep a post to do? This is the <u>third</u> time I have been sacked.

Mr. Ellis particularly bossy & tiresome today, taking over my grilling of the steak. I hide my nervousness, my immature inferiority-feeling, as best I can, but he upsets me. Then on top of that, he produced a heavy sack of peas 'to do in the afternoon'. I laughed & cried simultaneously.

### Thursday, July 13th

Dreadful day; gross inefficiency after gross inefficiency of mine discovered as the day went on. Get nastier & more bullying than ever. Think they are horrid beastly people. But I probably have made a bit too free with the Ellis's house, which also counts against me; I have eaten most of the cakes myself, as well as all my other ravages in the larder, stayed on in the guest room when they had told me in so many words I must move, used their soap in the bathroom, the man will have to come to see to the washing machine, I drink a good 'pinta' a day, have taken their bike in the rain, the plug of the iron broken . . .

**Friday, July 14th**

Drastically overslept this morning, didn't hear my alarm, & didn't wake till quarter to eight. It was a dreadful humiliation & had to rush round in a panic still in my night-clothes. Everything was in a dreadful mess, because hadn't time to clear up after the Ellis's party last night. My degeneration terrible . . . .

This morning, afraid Mr Ellis might

hit me

**Saturday, July 15th**

Left the Ellis's in utter ignominy and disgrace.

# 21 Oh, glorious blaze!

Will I soon be able to talk with fire?

**Aged twenty-two**

And so Laura was launched into adult life. She will try her hand at another housekeeping job. That will also go wrong. She is a disaster in the kitchen. It is absurd for her even to contemplate such work again. To her family she is a byword for clumsiness and domestic implosion. But at last she finds her way: she goes to London, secures a prestigious studentship at Camberwell College of Art – and we have arrived at the cheap black notebook covered in washable rexine that I picked out on the first day Dido gave me the diaries – the diary which announces a Great Project that <u>MUST BE DONE!!</u>

In the early 1960s people were racing out of Camberwell's doors to become actors, models, fashion gurus, sculptors, painters, potters, animators, pianists, publishers, textile designers and lead guitarists with Pink Floyd. Laura, studying illustration, surged with the crowd:

> Still in high excitement over Crystal Palace. Can still hardly believe it is <u>my</u> poster they like, <u>mine</u> that is chosen, mine, mine!!

'The artist is the highest-developed human being one can have,' she announces. 'Intellectuals are less highly developed.' She no longer wants to be a scholar; she hates science; she understands at last what E means by 'work, work, work'. The work must 'fill

& dominate my soul'. 'I must continue with this starving life I have at last entered into – the long, slogging hours with only a sandwich.' Her difficulties with swallowing are because she is a genius. 'The more gifted one is the heavier the price . . . such things artists have to suffer. People do not know of these things, do not see an artist from inside, as I do.'

> What torture the cellist Paul Tortelier's nerves must be – the man can't keep still a minute – such facial tics & jerks etc etc. What a thyroid.

Laura feels glad that she is not so gifted as he. 'I suffer enough as it is, through my gifts – they won't let one alone, can't release a minute, one is used up.' But she is not weak. 'Although I am a gentle, over-sensitive creature, am really a career girl type, more than domesticated; have a certain sophistication. Am ambitious, want to get on, to give of my work to the community; long to have it appreciated, & feel my worth . . . My work must get known, & give pleasure to others. – Although it is original, it is not exclusive, the layman can enjoy it.'

> Worked today across the road, standing at an impromptu easel concocted of a step ladder, planks, & string. It was fun, & aroused interest in the passing locals.

'Oh, glorious blaze of the imaginative world!'

## 22  I have been stuck in this room twenty one years . . .

Can see it undetermined what I will become –
1) a personality, a writer of merit, perhaps even fame
2) moderately successful normal person
3) a lonely, embittered spinster, whom no one likes,
& who has got nowhere in life – me, with
all my dreams & hopes.

**Aged eighteen**

'I have been stuck in this room twenty one years next February. It is as long as it took Moth & Pa to bring me up – my whole childhood and teenage years, and a bit extra. I was twenty one when we went to a shop in the main street in Bedford, and I chose that wireless.'

The diary that might have explained the significance of this radio was not in the haul that Richard and Dido rescued from the skip, and Laura never mentions the incident again, before or after this one note written in 1994.

On the way back from visiting Dido in the oncology ward at the Royal Free, I tested other words in place of 'wireless'.

'I was twenty one when we went to a shop in the main street in Bedford, and I chose that hammer and nail.' That 'grapefruit'. That 'stuffed toy rabbit'. That 'chicken'. Each time I changed the object, the image that I had of the type of shop and the display also changed, but the expression on Laura's face remained the same. Even though she was twenty-one at the time of the incident, a fully-grown adult of seven metres, in my mind it is a girl of about fourteen, watchful and tentative, who reaches out to pick up the prize. Her mother is standing closer behind her than her father. Her father is awkward and pompous. He has a fat belly and a thick nose. Her mother, though I feel I know her better, is indistinct – a presence, bent over; not a person.

Modern words also worked. I tried 'iPad'. As if puncturing through soap bubbles, Laura's fourteen-year-old hand stretched out to a shop shelf five decades in the future. Something, to my mind, has fixed her as a child trapped in an adult's body. It is not endearing. It is slightly nasty. I know several people like this: old women who are teenage boys; grown men who are twelve. They are children poured into old people's skins. Their bodies have aged but their brains have encountered a hitch.

I try 'Fluorouracil (5FU)', one of the three poisons the well-intentioned hospital is mainlining into Dido and which (it will turn out) are doing nothing much except hardening up the tumour and destroying her brain cells so that she can't write, can't think, can't read, can't edit, shits uncontrollably in nappies and has to keep a purple Really Useful plastic crate next to her bed into which she vomits twice an hour.

By 1994, Laura was fifty-five and close to suicide, but there is a mordancy about her grumbles. It's like listening to traffic: annoying but reassuring when your best friend is being savaged by illness and medical barbarity.

If I had an ounce of mercy or courage I would shoot Dido. I do not have an ounce of mercy.

I read Laura instead.

The two decades of 'imprisonment' Laura suffered at the end of her life, in what may or may not have been an asylum, subject to the control of this man Peter – her confinement wasn't absolute. She could leave her room and the house; but she was back on her mattress by the end of the day. She was allowed to attend her father's funeral, visit her mother (who, like so many ex-Cambridge University students, has ended up growing old near her former college, in Girton), shop for food and clothes, spend an afternoon in the cinema. 'Grinding' back and forth on her bike she visits the Co-op on Histon Road and purchases:

A 50p bunch of watercress that had started to rot,

A liver casserole ready meal, which she boiled up 'to make it safe',

Seven cauliflowers,

A fat-reduced garlic dip for 15p ('if it isn't nice, it isn't a disaster'),

The 'remains' of a swede,

Five kiwis in a packet that she found in a trolley waiting to be thrown out, and which the Co-op cashier insisted it was against the law to sell; but he charged her 10p for them anyway.

She drew the line at a bit of Stilton that had maggots in it, and took it back to the shop to complain. 'I was prepared to excuse one, but it had several.'

On one occasion, returning with a Rosamund Pilcher book bought from the market for a triumphantly small sum, we discover that although Laura detests Peter, she has attempted erotic thoughts about him:

> The story strained my credulity a bit. Knowing my
> experience of Peter, so horrible and pongy, etc. It is
> not really romantic – this woman walking into this
> man's bedroom first thing with the tea, and them
> making love. As if people feel like it, first thing.

Is she suffering from a mild version of Stockholm syndrome, in which hostages fall in love with their captors?

There are reasons to believe she might be in an asylum. The graphologist's comments suggest madness. Vince the detective suspects that the size of Laura's handwriting is a metaphor for imprisonment. Laura, in the days of The Phobia, thought she might be fundamentally insane. If she is in a prison for criminals, it must be a Category D, and she must be at least a quarter of the way through her full sentence, because only then are inmates allowed into the community. But I can say categorically that if these are the diaries of a mad woman or a convict, she was not incarcerated anywhere among the streets near where Richard and Dido found the books. The Arts and Crafts houses in that neighbourhood are reserved for the captains of academic industry: heads of department, retired vice chancellors of the university, the older generation of multimillionaires who made their money in computers. Wittgenstein died in the house on the corner called, blissfully, 'Storey's End'. Each one of these widely separated properties has the acreage and oaken stillness of a national archive. There are no bang-ups here, at least not official ones.

The houses in Storey's Way are hidden behind bushes.

The neighbours are unworldly.

It would be easy for an unofficial gaoler to convince people here that a middle-aged woman's cries for help were nothing remarkable. You could say that what had just been overheard was you listening to your old reel-to-reel research recordings of the call of *Gracula religiosa*, the famous 'talking bird' from the Nicobar islands.

Then you would stroll back inside, pausing to reposition a dahlia stake on the way, and drag your victim to a room that was deeper in the house.

Over the years, small but suspicious details about Peter emerge. He has a passion for grapefruit slices. He never finishes bottles of milk. He does not wash his hands after peeing. He is blandly well off, and never does anything interesting with his money – he once hid £30,000 worth of his stamp collection in a hole somewhere in the garden, and forgot where the hole was. He never found those little sticky bits of paper again. As in the case of Josef Fritzl, the Austrian who trapped his daughter in the family basement for twenty-four years, Peter trained as an electrical engineer. He mows the grass until it bleeds.

I imagine Peter as a short but energetic man, with a limp and an unexplained swing of his arm as he walks along, mentally lopping off those dahlia heads. On the mowing machine, his knuckles are white from wrenching at the steering wheel. I see him spin round the pear trees, a freshly opened tin of grapefruit slices on the bonnet (he liked the giant size, enough for twelve servings), and race up the lawn through the bonfire smoke.

But Peter is never clearly defined. Even the way his name keeps popping up and disappearing on the page has something furtive about it. He is never caught in the act of doing anything; he has always either done it five minutes ago or will do it again in twelve hours. This gives the strange effect that he seems to be as aware of our presence as we are of his, and therefore confines his bad behaviour to the moments when we turn the page. By the time we have pressed the next side down, regained our focus and begun to read again, it is too late: the lawnmower is back in the shed and another bag of Laura's photographs and sheet music roaring on the garden fire.

He is, according to the diaries, in his early seventies and worth between five and twelve million pounds.

She is not his prisoner.

She is his live-in housekeeper.


Of all the jobs, how on earth did messy, dreamy, impractical, hopeless cook and artistic snob Laura land this one? Following her abysmal performance in the Wirral, what made her think of applying for it? It was precisely to escape this type of work that she had fled to Camberwell. Working as a housekeeper-companion for a bachelor professor is a domestic situation that belongs in the nineteenth century. She does his supper, his washing up, his shopping, his cleaning. She sometimes helps with the gardening; they frequently have meals together, occasionally even breakfast. She is, as she frequently points out, his wife – without the sex ('thank goodness').

The late diaries with the merry coloured covers are a long howl of protest against this glutinous existence. When Peter is away, which is not often enough, she plays Mozart and Beethoven on the grand piano in his living room and weeps over her wasted life. Once, at the Co-op on Christmas Eve, she spots his bicycle leaned up against the window:

> I couldn't resist giving the basket a push – the basket is starting to break up in any case, so I just pushed the rest of the side in. I hoped it would make it difficult for the bleeder to get the shopping home – but he <u>still</u> got back long before me, must have gone slipping home . . .

In her eagerness to damage his bicycle she forgot to pick up anything in the Co-op for herself, and ended up celebrating Christmas that year with 'one packet of stewing turkey'.

Another time she assaults his furniture:

> My excessive tension no indication of happiness here on my part – but yet can't bear to leave – the thought of other jobs, or going home, still worse. I am so irresponsible that I am starting to smash the place up – I also reduced that chair of Peter's to matchwood the other day. I also set about with the poker, belabouring other articles – wished for an axe . . . I am not even a wife to this man Peter – am nothing, just a caretaker, who has vandalised his property!

That entry covers twenty-four hours without sleep and takes up thirty pages.

> There was an article in the local paper last night about low pay – I see how astonishingly I have fallen behind – that even women are getting very much more in ordinary jobs; and men get as much in a week as I get in a whole month.

Why did she take this job? The dead diarist never tells us, but to me the explanation is clear. I blame the letter E.

## 23  Who E?

Rather flattered that E thought me a human-being.
**Aged twenty-one**

Laura was fourteen until she was thirty; sixty until she was forty, and better kept in the spare room from then on.

The cause of this peculiar ageing process was E.

E first crops up in the diaries when Laura had her job at the public library, but their first meeting occurred six years earlier. Laura was fourteen, and hadn't yet moved to Whitefield House and become a pupil at the Perse School for Girls. It was the period of the oldest volume in the collection, the school exercise book dated 1952 with the central pages showing three ghostly sketches of a girl slumped against the keys of a piano, apparently in despair, and the back pages cut out using a razor. Laura was still living with her parents ('not exploratory spirits – the search for truth is a dead area to them') in Tudor Cottage.

E came to the house as her piano teacher.

He was kind, supportive, interesting, dogmatic, good enough (he says) to be a concert pianist and grotesquely irresponsible. He allowed a young girl's adulation to get out of hand.

E sees the world in terms of buckets – that's my interpretation. To each person, a bucket. A bucket is made up of one's natural endowments, societal responsibilities and the application of hard work. The ordinary person has no endowments, many responsibilities and is concerned only with staying alive; such a person will never rise above a quarter of a bucketful of life. The Great Artist has a full bucket. What's more, his genius is evident from an early age, he works like a galley slave and his societal duty is to produce Art. Society's duty in return is to accept and encourage the Artist and not mind too much about the mess and occasional nastiness that spills from an overloaded bucket. E is an example of this type of bucket. He has considerable natural gifts (the piano, those poems he'd had published); his talent appeared early; he has worked exceptionally hard. But in his case society has failed to applaud him. He is an unrecognised bucket. He will soon be a bucket of bitterness.

Scientists are not worth thinking about. Nobody cares about their buckets.

Laura is mid-bucket. When we first met her properly, working in the public library in 1958, she still needed adult instruction; she had perhaps found her talent (writing – although it might have been drawing, or maybe symphonic music, but it could be song-writing and is probably opera), and though already nineteen she was, as E points out with unstinting helpfulness, foolish and stupid and couldn't make her big body stand up straight. That's why he fills up his bucket cheeks and blows Esaids at her:

> E disapproved of my new handbag.
> E ticked me off for lack of dress sense.
> E said men are on the whole better at cooking than women.
> E said 'yes, it is bitter.'

The reason Laura left her parents' house in Luton to go to school at the Perse Girls, in Cambridge, was because E had got a post as an extra-curricular music teacher there. Laura was not academically attentive enough to attend the Perse Girls; her parents could not afford to send her to the Perse Girls; there was no reason why she should go to the Perse Girls; yet Laura determined that she would go to the Perse Girls and so she did go to the Perse Girls. It was perhaps the last time in her life that Laura displayed resolve.

Laura frequently mentions that E is Jewish, from Berlin or Vienna (it turns out to be Bonn). In middle age, she admits that the reason she is so eager to watch the Tour de France on television is because she thinks one of the cyclists must be related to E. This sportsman's name is Bobby Julich.

E is therefore E. Julich.

In Cambridge, he lived here:

Which is, believe it or not, a Grade II listed building. Sometimes when Laura visits E in the evening she cannot see where he is sitting in the large rooms of his apartment because he is fussy about electricity. Laura has to grope around in semi-darkness. She knows he is in here somewhere, she can sense him watching her. She can distinguish the blackness of the grand piano and feel the edges of the tables and chairs covered in crackly newspaper, but the only light in the room comes from street lamps behind the trees outside and the buses passing by on their way to and from the train station. However, E is never able to hide himself for long. Even in the dark his viciousness shines bright.

> E said I am a 'silly ass'.
> E said I am stupid.
> E said I am 14 years old [this written when she was twenty]. I am not ripe enough yet.
> E said I shouldn't live in London because of being raped.
> E said I was weak in every way.
> E kept saying I am a weakling. E said there is no place for them in life, they ought to be hung up.

Why did Laura love this abysmal man? Although later she would be amazed by her thraldom, during the late 50s and early 60s she viewed E as more central to her being than she was herself. Laura was a robot directed by E; Laura was an E-shaped carcass.

> Was aware of that feeling of me being a dead personality beside E.

At the risk of getting too lit. crit. about this, E was both E and 'I'.

If only Laura's subjection had not been so mingled with eroticism!

> E told me I am stupid in my ideas about money.
> *Feel E loves me for my mistakes.*
> E said 'I can hardly take any more of the things you say, they're so stupid.'

*Loved E terribly, E so loving & understanding & c feely &*
*sweet. Hugged myself for rapture over E.*
E put a hand on my arm, & told me seriously I had
received such a lot of good advice, if only I'd taken it,
goodnight.
*Dreamt very sexily of E last night, I think of mouthing E*
*on a bed, and the sexy feeling went over to my waking*
*hours, found E even more desirable than usual.*
E said lifts seldom go wrong.

There is also a sense in which E is quite right. Until Laura is
thirty she is a neurotic, petulant, lazy, delusional girl who
never, outside of those few years at Camberwell, sits down to
work:

> E said I don't have the mental powers to go to
> university. E didn't believe in any of my so-called gifts,
> not even writing.
> E said terrible things. Didn't know whether I can work.
> E (head in hands in despair) said 'I don't know.'

The self-conscious sensitivity of people who have been 'good at
English' at school has in Laura become corrupted almost into
insanity. Even without E, this un-industrious worship of her
artistic self could explain why Laura went wrong.

Laura, aged fourteen, was a typical schoolgirl who loved arty
things and wanted to be a triumphant arty sort of person and
was good (sometimes very good) at writing and drawing and not
bad at the piano. Along comes E. Julich, potential concert
pianist, and tangles up Laura's ambition with a schoolgirl crush.

But then Laura did not develop into any sort of artist at all, because she didn't work at it. She didn't know how to. She was just another one of those silly people who says 'Everyone's got a book in them,' or 'I could write a book if I had the time,' and so never gets anywhere. For Laura, Art is not something you have to grind, file and strop. That's what she calls 'materialism'. To Laura, a young teenager, Art is eroticism.

> E said [my] song-capacity, nothing, just a manifestation of the sexual impulse, like the singing of the birds & animals.

And Laura becomes a failure not just at Art but at life, just as E – the great pianist, the published poet, the ... er (so humiliating) A-Level music supply teacher – feels he has become. What happened after that was not part of a deliberate policy by E, but it has the feel of an inevitability. E's support turned to vindictiveness. He tried to crush Laura, his second failed self, and succeeded.

The only thing Laura ever applies herself to is her diary.

Her Great Project, whether she intended it to be or not, is not her art, or a new symphony, or an invention that's now so common that I might be using it at this minute without realising it; it's these books.

But you have to be careful. Most people sound unbalanced in their diaries (if those diaries are honest), because that's one of their purposes: to let out unspeakable things for a little runaround.

There are, however, two facts I have definitely got wrong in my cynical interpretation of Laura's life and E's role in its collapse. I have just spotted them in a red notebook with black speckles dated 1961. The first is that E was ...

a woman.

Two, she was . . .

seventy-two years old.

## 24 Despite the fact that time passes with treacle-like languor . . .

I who am always young will inevitably be old.

**Aged eighteen**

Despite the fact that time passes with treacle-like languor in the late, colourful diaries, they are compelling to read. Perhaps it is precisely because of the featurelessness that the narrative is so gripping: the story becomes as open to improbabilities as a fantasy.

Not that anything does happen.

Nothing ever happens.

*I had reheated cauliflower stalks for supper*

I had reheated cauliflower stalks for supper

she writes from her bed one Friday night in June.

I <u>do</u> prefer cauliflower stalks, even reheated ones,
to oranges and strawberries

she adds two pages on. Three days – 7,632 words – away from that: Shock news! Hold the front page!

*I have just started a new cauliflower.*

> I have just started a new cauliflower.

She is not perfectly monovegetabic. She enjoys other food. On June 4th, she savours a memory about radishes:

> I treated myself to radishes two days ago which were 69p for only about nine radishes.

But then she hesitates. There is something wrong about this recollection. For a moment she cannot figure it out.

> It may only have been seven radishes, I can't quite remember.

Reading Laura's entries in the 1990s is like listening to a tomb breathe.

But still you want to go on reading. It took me several years to understand the obvious reason why these pages are gripping.

I had moved again, and was living in Suffolk. It was October, the start of the shooting season. Several of the woods around the house I was renting had home-made chairs in them for culling deer, lashed to the trunks of big oaks. These seats were about twelve feet above the ground, with a ladder attached. The gamekeeper could perch here quietly above the flow of scent, out of sight, and when he fired, the single bullet passed safely through the brain of the passing animal into the earth behind.

One morning, sitting in one of these chairs working on a diary from the late 1990s, I heard a leafy unwrapping sound and looked down to see eight deer grazing at my feet. They had crept up on me without either them or me knowing. I had been too absorbed in reading; they, in grass. There was a shallow mist and just their heads were above the vapour, trophies before their time. They moved slowly and in silence, dipping their faces in and out of the obscurity to nibble at the ground. Several were small; only their ears showed above the mist. After ten minutes they wandered off, crackling softly between the trees.

It was as I was walking back, ecstatic, through the mud that I realised why I wanted to keep reading Laura's diary entries, even when they are agonisingly tedious. It is because they are true.

Nothing exciting had happened with the deer. They had just been there, true things, thinking themselves alone. Laura is also a true thing. No novelist has clattered in to impose a narrative 'arc' on the images of incarceration and waste in these books; she has not obscured the truth in balanced sentences and well-chosen words. Without the crank of a managed structure that a fiction writer (or a biographer, for that matter) would need to force on Laura's story nothing is off the point and anything is possible; yet the fact that drama never happens is not disappointing. With Laura you are alone with a woman who thinks she is alone – a woman in the final stages of tedium. She has absolutely no awareness of your presence. Her drama is that she is not fiction.

In physics there is no specialness about 'now'. The physicist's picture of the world encompasses the entire sweep from future to past. The junction between the two, that minuscule ring of the present that matters so much to us, has no distinctive theoretical role. In Laura's diaries from the 1990s, the situation is the inverse: only 'now' is clear; only 'here', in this room, tonight, matters. A TV show might provoke thoughts about the past, but it is the act of having those thoughts, not the past itself, that she wants to record. Everything that this woman locked up in her bedroom late in the evening writes, and by writing makes interesting, could be replaced by a single, endlessly repeated, mysterious sentence: I am alive. I am alive. I am alive . . .

When she is not shopping, cooking, dusting, washing up, negotiating with the milkman, bickering with the cleaner, the gardener, herself –

> Going to be a mouse no longer – jolly well might tell Betty I won't have her doing the kitchen on Fridays when I'm cooking; & tell Evans not to grow sprouts always. Shall tell Peter the truth about my 'fit of spleen'. It's about time he knew how I really feel about things. Bloody well am going to be a musician too, & will play Mozart with an orchestra if I want to.

– mopping the floor, picking apples, emptying the garbage, changing sheets, defrosting the fridge, filling the washing machine, handwashing woollens or writing her diary, Laura watches TV.

For twenty-five years.

> I felt very depressed when I woke up this morning – reality hitting me again, last night's enjoyment evaporated. The TV is like a drug, and prevents me thinking . . . If I had had a TV when I was in digs, I might have been less likely to break down. It makes such an enormous difference, to have it. It is also nice before lunch.

She is never going to be a musician, because she never thinks of herself as a musician first. She is always a house-keeper, then a person, then a musician. I'm the same about physics. To me, the only subject worth anything is physics. By comparison, writing is pathologically self-obsessed, emotionally trite and meretricious. Physics is intellectual work; writing is part of the entertainment industry. This is why writers tend to be boring people, and scientists not. But I will never be a physicist, because I think of myself as a biographer first, a human second, and a physicist never. The opening trick to becoming is to convince yourself that you already are. Laura and I both fall at the first hurdle.

Everything about Laura's writing in these colourful books from the 1990s suggests constriction. From the 1960s to the 1980s, she was a remarkably diligent diarist; now she's an obsessive one. Each book, containing between 120,000 and 150,000 words, is filled in two months. The 'o's and 'a's have almost disappeared into themselves; they are punctured balls. The 's's at the ends of words have shrivelled into tails. The 'd's are still deltas, rather haughty; the dangly-down bit on the 'y' still shoots back as if it's been thwacked with a bat. But these flourishes now seem like releases instead of ornaments, as though Laura needs to use up the ink she's squeezed away from the other letters. Meanwhile, the words pour in until the page is done, then she turns over and begins again.

The passage of time is still clear, but the calendar has started to disappear: few of the later books mention what year they were written, sometimes not even what month.

In the 1970s and 1980s, Laura spent her free time going on careless bike rides in the country; 'slaying' Schumann preludes on her employer's piano; taking week-long holidays to Rottingdean with E, where they argued about who stole the butter in the night.

After 1990 everything succumbs to television. Laura's idea of bliss is to sweep her boss out the front door, boil up a pack of Vesta chicken curry (which is so corrosive that when she's not eating it she uses it to clean egg off the saucepan) and spend three weeks ogling doped-up men in Lycra battle over the Pyrenees in the Tour de France. If it is the Queen's day at Ascot or there's a royal wedding, she won't even go into town to cash her pay cheque from Peter, although she is always overdrawn. When E lies dying in London, it is because she wants to see more French bicycle racing that Laura refuses to visit her. She disappears as a human being during these last years, and reappears as a 2-D reflection on the TV screen.

From the biographer's point of view, it's a big improvement.

In the earliest books, Laura rarely tells anecdotes, reports dialogue or gives descriptions of people she's met. Her interest is to transcribe the burble of her obsessions. After 1990 unexpected biographical breakthroughs appear because of the television. In 1998, *Pet Rescue* on Channel 4 features a dog called Buster who is sent to a rich house where the woman cooks him a supper of fried steak and carrots, served on a plate 'like a hotel'. The event is so shocking to Laura, so cleanly contemptible, that for a moment she is taken back forty years:

> It was a better dinner than I get myself . . . really, the food Auntie Doll did for the dogs at Whiters was ideal. She did a side of horsemeat for them, and used to cut bits off every day, and give it with biscuits.

Where do you store a side of horse in 1962? Laura doesn't say. Pretty Auntie Doll pops up like a medieval monster, makes a savage attack on a dead horse, and is gone.

In 2000, on an episode of *Antiques Roadshow* (BBC 1) broadcast from Penshurst Place, Laura spots that the Elizabethan poet and courtier Sir Philip Sidney

*looked rather like Uncle John*

looked rather like Uncle John.

She remembers that Sidney might be

*some sort of cousin*

some sort of cousin.

'If the ancestors of the Whitersites once lived at Penshurst
Place . . . my distant family was entertaining Henry VIII, even.'

'It was really good of Sidney to give water to a dying man
like that, instead of having it himself,' she adds fondly.

As in all the diaries, Laura's sense of self comes from
comparing herself to other people. With art and music a
failure, TV has become the measure of herself.

Unable to sleep one night, she fishes around her room
and finds Enid Blyton's schoolgirl novel, *Summer Term
at St Clare's*:

> It's stunning, it's marvellous. It seems to bring me greater
> joy as an adult than it did as a child. I got as far as Janet
> is hauled over the coals by Miss Roberts for going to the
> cinema, when I needed to get up to go to the lavatory –
> left the book with a groan. To lie sleepless all night in
> bed, straining my eyes, has been a kind of happiness;
> I thought of nothing but this happy enthralling world
> of girlhood. The book, incidentally, was 15 pence –
> that little merit was thought of it – whilst rubbish in the
> bookshop sells for pounds. Can't help thinking that
> Uncle Wick's heavy treatise on Macedonia (at £25 a
> volume) is rubbish compared with this delightful little
> work of art.

From which we learn that her uncle was Nicholas Geoffrey Lemprière Hammond CBE DSO, author of *Philip of Macedon*; *The Macedonian State: The Origins, Institutions and History*; *History of Macedonia* (three volumes); and (in case he hasn't made his life's purpose quite clear) *History of Macedonia* (one volume). Laura calls him 'Uncle Wick'.

Was her name Laura Hammond?

I pushed the question aside. I liked this woman whatever her name. I enjoyed her clumsiness and her obsessions and her occasional desires for an outburst of violence. I thought I recognised a lot of her qualities in myself. I wanted to understand her. Biographers often report that they enjoy a private relationship with their subject that is, impossibly, acknowledged on both sides. Dido talked about it frequently when she was writing her biography of the comic novelist William Gerhardie, who died five years before she began her work. So what if Laura's last name was Hammond? We had got beyond last-name terms.

Laura frequently uses quotation marks in these books to hold certain terms apart from the rest of the sentence. Often these are clichés, or modern turns of phrase, or words she evidently thinks are vulgar or commercial, and so the quotes show that she has adopted the correct ironic detachment. 'To "do one's best" '; 'mother is not very good at "taping" things'; 'the "safety-pin youth" '; ' "God" not quite "delivered", after all'.

'God' always gets plucked out this way, but so do 'yoghurts'.

There is not always a suggestion of wryness, and she's not being purely snobbish either. Frequently, the quotes surround the name of a TV programme or celebrity: 'Father Ted', 'Alan Titchmarsh', 'Oz Clarke', 'Dame Edna Everage'. But she does the same for 'Nicholas Nickleby'. These names get singled out because they are larger-than-life figures. Their days are so dramatic and hot compared to her own that they have to be handled with quotation-shaped tongs.

Michael Barrymore doesn't get this treatment, however, even though he's the most preposterous real-life character of all. Laura loves Michael Barrymore like a disreputable younger brother.

> There is a small bulletin on Barrymore in the Sun – he 'strenuously denies' the allegations that he followed the 27 year old youth into the basement toilets. I feel sorry for Barrymore, I must say. He was so nice about it, when the tortoise in the show ruined his suit.

Chopin, Mozart, Beethoven and Rosemary West, the serial killer, are also never put in quotes.

> I think if one saw Rose West in M&S, one would be able to see she wasn't right in the head.

Laura's read and watched so much about these sociopaths and geniuses that they've shaken off their inverted commas. They've become mirrors of herself. By spotting shared characteristics with Barrymore or Beethoven she establishes that she has some existence outside her appalling room. She squeezes under the door, throws off her fears and lives everywhere:

> My life would be very, very different indeed, if I was the BBC Food and Drink presenter Jilly Goolden.

Although it's difficult to see what other objects are in her housekeeper's quarters apart from the television set, occasionally Laura complains about 'the terrible ache in my eyes' and turns her attention away from the screen so we can look around.

The room is not on the ground floor. There is a window near the bed that looks down on the house orchard. If she leans out far enough she can see across a field owned by the Veterinary School to the Ascension Parish graveyard, where Wittgenstein is buried. At night, she can watch the moon arc slowly over the roofs of Churchill College.

> It really is strange, that there seem to be things on the moon, relics of a civilisation of giants. There is a crane that has a boom 25 miles long! There is a sort of chandelier thing, and a thing rather like the Eiffel tower . . .

The ceiling in her room is high. The walls are wainscoted. There is a bedside table with a clock that she believes she can 'remote view', i.e. tell the time on it without looking, as CIA operatives were supposedly trained to do in the Cold War. Next to the clock is a box of Mogadon and another of aspirin and a mug of Horlicks.

On the floor there are always several paperbacks. Almost all are novels, biographies or true crime.

We know that Laura hates her own reflection, and therefore we can guess that there are no mirrors on the walls of her bedroom. She never cuts her luxuriant hair herself even though she could save money that way, and she always wants to save money.

> I had to wait a bit at the hairdressers, I must say how much I hated how I looked, in the big mirror; probably fatter than last year; and there might be something in it, when E used to say I have a 'round face' and 'like a full moon'.

Adding a moon-shaped jaw solves the boxer-in-a-wig problem, but it makes Laura look deranged. The difficulty is with the eyes (if you cover the eyes, the mouth is pleasant). I've been infected by the mania of the later writing, and I am not good enough at drawing to get rid of it. This is the mask of her young face stretched over her middle-aged diaries.

She puts off buying smalls until her current underwear has fallen apart because she doesn't want to see her reflection in the changing room.

> Make a note; that I made another attempt to get a bra at M&S. I tried on three, in separate stages. It really was exhausting, having to get undressed three times.

Even when she does find something that fits, the acknowledgement of what she has become means she won't pay for it.

> I nearly did buy the bra that was 42B . . . In my early years at Peter's I used to have a 38B.

Flora insists that all the humps I've drawn between Laura's
arms as a result of this new bra information are not right

We also know that there is at least one radiator present,
because just as the weather starts to get cold, Pongy Peter
sneaks in when she isn't looking and turns it off. Six months
later, as soon as the outside temperature returns to 26 degrees,
he creeps back and turns the radiator on again.

One of the oddities of looking round a room by the light of
a private diary is that the more precise the description of an
object, the less likely that it is actually there. It's not interesting

to th...
missi...
photog
the roo...
sonatas ...
in that pi...
suspects, ...
to be chara

I wasr...

When I thi...
in bed, late at ...
but not very ple...
lying full stretch
head is hemmed
Peter's brutalised

Nov. 25th. Saddens me beyond words to th...
young, gay president lying beneath ins...
...the river o...
knowing no more than ...

Nov. 26th. America's trage...
left of the President ex...
people; and I thin...
ignited, 'that ...
its messa...

...ole, and at the top end by a maho... ...that looms up into the dark. The TV is glo...ing and flickering at her feet as if someone is hurriedly trying to complete a welding project, and beyond that, barely visible in the jolting shadows, are the teetering piles of brilliantly-coloured notebooks: the triumphs of a scribbled-down life.

November 22nd, 1963, a third of a century earlier. BANG! Kennedy assassinated: Single bullet. 350 metres. It's one of the few occasions in any of the diaries, late or early, that the outside world penetrates the self-obsessed fog. The poignancy of the young President's funeral upsets her entries for six days.

Bedtime:– Feel very sorry for Jackie Kennedy tonight; no longer the First Lady in the land, but the loneliest lady in the land.

nk of the

nsate earth,

the flowers.

ly still makes me cry; nothing

cept his spirit in the hearts of the

of the eternal flame that Jackie has

ill henceforth always flutter and twinkle

ge to the capital city across the Potomac River'.

ov. 28th. The world moving on now, and mourning put
aside. Poor Jackie is already fading into obscurity; will be
busy now, arranging a move of house . . .

This is the last major political event mentioned in the books
that I've read. Since then, four million words: nothing.

Watergate scandal, Lebanese civil war, Margaret Thatcher.
Not a mention.

Bhopal gas leak, fall of the Berlin Wall, bombing of the
World Trade Center.

Not a peep.

There is one letter in the handwriting that has not changed
between the early diaries and these late colourful ones. It is
always put down with care and given respectful, unnecessary
end bars which would have slowed the pace of the script
noticeably. But with this letter there is no compromise. It is
the capital letter 'I'.

# 25  Who E? (cont.)

> It is rather as if I were on my bicycle – bicycling
> along merrily, and then a car passes too close, so
> that I wobble; so that if I'm not careful, I'll fall
> off all together, out of fright. That is an analogy –
> E's criticisms being the passing car.
>
> **Aged thirty-five**

To get away from the living is easy, but the dead follow you everywhere. There's no escaping an absence.

It took Laura twenty years to recover from the death of E in 1979. She developed agoraphobia; she had a breakdown; she turned into a hoarder. The clutter in her room, mostly 10p trinkets brought back from charity shops, became catastrophic. It was to make a dent in this mountain that Peter had taken to sneaking in, carving off portions, and having a 'burn up' on the bonfire. He isn't to be condemned too harshly. When she attacked Peter's furniture in the middle of the night and made deep stab marks in the living-room door with a knife, he let it pass. They had known each other for half of Laura's life. They had loved and lost several people in that time.

There was never any sex between Laura and E. Julich in the thirty years they knew each other. Their affair was always what it had been at the start: a schoolgirl crush. When E died, Laura lost her closest friend, her mentor, her decision-maker, her personification of artistry and, for the next twenty years, herself.

The fact that E has turned out to be an elderly woman doesn't change my interpretation of the way she ruined Laura's life, but it has made me more sympathetic. I want to know the details – how does a sixty-four-year-old female seduce a fourteen-year-old girl? How can E, placed in front of an attractive, heterosexual, independent teenager, turn her own wrinkles and white hair into such searing erotic beauty that she brings the girl to her knees?

I have to say, now that I know the answer, I wish I'd met E. The woman deserves respect.

She did it with a sonata.


Beethoven's *Pathétique* is a work of repeated assaults. It opens with a crash.

To my ear, music that starts like this means the pianist should panic, slam down the keyboard cover and let the notes finish bumping about on their own. But immediately afterwards, the *Pathétique* hits quietness.

The notes that follow are a lull between breakers; they feel as if they shouldn't be trusted. And they shouldn't . . . Bang! The big noise comes again; then more quietness.

'You've heard of Gieseking, of course? Walter Gieseking?' said Graeme Mitchison, jolting open his front door. Graeme is the only pianist I know. He has two concert grands slotted back to back in his drawing room, but how they got there is impossible to understand. They could not have fitted through the doors or windows. A strong set of bookshelves juts out from the wall behind one of these pianos and contains hundreds of stern-looking scores with titles that suggest the deeper parts of a German car engine: *Klavierstücke, Präludien und Fugen, Band Zwei*. You can see an unfortunate picture of Graeme on Twitter, playing in the portrait gallery of the Fitzwilliam Museum in Cambridge: 'Amazing lunchtime concert'. He looks as if he's driving one of Peter's large lawnmowers. He seems a little cross. There appears to be a piece of marble pressing down the piano lid. Has he grabbed it from the sculpture gallery?

'Not heard of Gieseking?' Graeme bobbed backwards in surprise. 'No, of course not, quite right, quite right.'

Gieseking turns out to have been a famous pianist. Another German, like E.

'The reason I mention him is because he used the same sonata to seduce me.'

I have been friends with Graeme for twenty-five years, but in many ways I don't know him at all. I know nothing about his private life. I know few of his friends. Startled by his confession, I squeezed up to a chair beside his grands and sat down.

'And this Gieseking – he was also much older than you?' I asked at last.

'Oh yes. Much older. Almost dead. It was wonderful.'

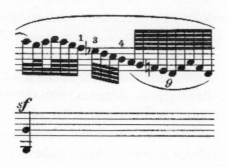

*Pathétique* does not mean 'pathetic' in a French accent. It comes from 'sympathetic' – it is an appeal to shared emotions.

'It was with this intense, contrasting opening movement that Gieseking caught me,' said Graeme. 'It would have been the same for Laura. I was in the attic of my parents' house. You said this woman E invited Laura to her house?'

'Her bedsit. She was a German refugee. Not much money.'

'Yes, that would have been better than an attic. It is a piece for the troubled soul. The great contrasts in the intensity of the chords, all the clashing, the titanic forces, the thrilling rustle of activity, the dynamics going from *fortissimo* down to *pianissimo* . . . and to think Laura heard it live, whereas my seduction was just a recording. An old 78 that my parents had stored out of the way. It started me practising seriously, and I have never stopped since.'

I listened intently as Graeme performed the piece. He played, I am sure, gloriously.

It did nothing for me.

With the slow decline of Dido I have come to find romantic music irritating – pop or classical, grand like the *Pathétique* or gentle like Chopin. It wants to barge its way into places where feelings are complex and subtle, and substitute a summary. Precisely what appealed to Graeme and Laura when they were fourteen is what I, nearing fifty, hate about it: its power, in Graeme's words, 'to reflect something that is going on in the world, take it, codify it, remove it from the area of chaos'. Such music is like clingfilm to my mind: it stretches across your tumbled mood, missing out the smaller bumps, suffocating everything by its attempt to sympathise with and represent the world of your disordered feelings. It makes me feel a little ill. When I do listen to classical music these days, the only type I can face is stuff that doesn't attempt to ambush you emotionally. I've discovered it by riffling through Flora's CD collection. Renaissance composers with bouncy names: Monteverdi, Gesualdo. The notes in their music sound to me pleasantly chilly.

'But why? Why *exactly*?' I pressed Graeme. 'If I'm Laura listening to you perform this sonata, why do I fall in love with you? If there's a book I think is magical and marvellous, I don't fall in love with the author. I never want to look at the photo of who's written a book. Authors are horrible to look at. Why is it different for pianists – especially since they're not even doing their own work, they're performing someone else's creation? Instead of E, why didn't she form an obsession for Beethoven?'

'Because E was playing to her personally. You're a troubled teenage girl and you walk into the room and a concert pianist begins to perform this to you alone, just to you, on a grand piano – *obviously* you're going to fall in love!'


Reading her diary later, Laura must have felt she would never capture E. The words were there, written down – E's own words, present and correct, just as she had said them – but never the proper flavour of the woman; and when Laura returned to her memory to recollect what she had missed, the essential sense of E had already gone from there too. Laura needed to leap on her bicycle and ride off to visit E again.

> Expect her fascination will draw me to her like a
> magnet, even tomorrow, probably just to trail about
> with her in the path of car-bonnets, & be told I am
> weak willed, or need clean underwear.

To fix E to the page, Laura had to repeat the woman's demoral-ising criticisms in a chant.

> E said I have no common sense.
> E said I must overcome my allergy to people.
> E said I don't learn by my mistakes like others, because
> I always return to them, like my posture.

Sententious remarks, with an identical meaning but slightly
different word order, were recorded as if they were new
revelations. It was like trying to hold water in with bars:

> E said I'm stupid.
> E said I am stupid.
> E said how stupid I was.
> E said she had rarely encountered someone so stupid.
> E said I'm stupid.

Laura catalogued these shameful judgements as though they
were the results of a lab experiment, unquestionable, hinting at
a great truth, inconclusive. She was unable to capture the
fascination of the person behind them. Her diary pages, full of
E's viciousness, were (for her, if not the reader) empty of E.

In the mid-1970s Laura fell briefly in love with a second
woman. This is Dame Harriette, the eminent ninety-nine-year-
old microbiologist first mentioned nine chapters ago.

Harriette was another manipulative old character with
quiet sexual ways. Their relationship (from Laura's side) was
superficial, ecstatic, painful, startling but not disgusting –
another schoolgirl crush. From Harriette's point of view,
Laura was barely there.

> As usual, longed to press my lips to the old woman's
> forehead etc.
> My love for her made me feel thrilled and excited, and
> I forgot to turn the tap of the hose off.
> My birthday tomorrow, and I may demand a kiss
> from little Harriette, if I have the guts.

> My birthday, and perhaps the most uncelebrated I have
> ever had! Little Harriette wished me well – but she
> hasn't given me anything!
> The old woman is subhuman and a psychopath.

'It is,' wrote Laura after tussling with another exhausting
sequence of emotional ups and downs while she worked for this
ancient person, 'really like being with a child, but a
sensible older child – one of ten, perhaps.'

I don't like Dame Harriette. She has a kittenish manner and
Laura is a mouse. The only time Laura doesn't see her as the
pinnacle of goodness is when she spots her as the nadir of bad.

For pages the two old women battle it out. Sometimes it is
almost impossible to figure out which one Laura's talking
about. E is central to Laura's life by precedent and out of Laura's
sense of loyalty; but then Dame Harriette is so much 'sweeter',
so 'adorable', so 'kissable'. In the confusion, Laura lets slip E's
first name: Elsa.

Elsa Julich. It's a difficult name to say. The 'a' of Elsa sets your
cheeks off in the wrong direction, and they have to switch and
hurry back to say that 'J'; the last two syllables clash.

Elsa Julich doesn't appear on the internet as a concert pianist
or a poet. There is an Elsa Julich who fled the Nazis in 1934,
but she was an internationally famous soprano who died in
Israel in 1964, at which time our Elsa was an enraged part-time
music teacher living on the edge of the Fens, still energetically
stamping on Laura's character.

> E said I look dreadful.
> E said I didn't seem to be liked very much.
> E said 'I know what a fool you are.'
> E said she might not always be right.

Does Graeme's musical analysis of Laura's early mental state change my ideas about Elsa's role in Laura's unhappy life? Perhaps. If Laura was already so deeply 'troubled' before she met Elsa (a period for which there are no diaries) that the pathos of a twenty-minute piece of music could be critical in trapping her forever, then Laura was going to go wrong with or without Elsa's predatory appearance. Yet the essential form of Elsa's cruelty – the exploitation of a schoolgirl crush, the outrage at Laura's refusal to be moulded in Elsa's image, the vituperative criticisms because she has failed to give Elsa a second shot at artistic excitement – they are the same.

But perhaps I've been too harsh. Elsa was always adamant that Laura must continue to attend to her studies when Laura joined the Cambridge city library after leaving the Perse Girls (we are back in 1958–59 now). Elsa encouraged Laura to work harder, to pay more attention in her secretarial classes and to rein in her obsession with writing 'Clarence' novels and drawing 'Clarence' cartoon strips; in other words, to stop being so dreamy and hormonal. And Elsa does admit to frailties now and then. That always gave Laura a pleasurable tremble:

> E said she doesn't get afraid of things.
> E said there have been times in her life when she's been terribly afraid.
> E said she was afraid when she was alone in that big house in Germany during the war with just one child, expecting bombs to be dropped on the house.
> E said when she meets another person alone on a country walk she is afraid; once, when E saw someone coming towards her, she turned, & went back.

And for a couple of lines – about seven seconds at the speed

Laura writes – she gloats with a sense of existing independently of Elsa. 'That amazed & thrilled me – fancy E of all people, of such courage & nobility, having such a weakness, the same unwarranted feeling I would get in the circumstances. I could hardly hide my joy and exaltation over having E being so sweet to me, & saying such lovely things . . . I adored E madly, and liked myself too.'

She cycled away from Elsa's flat triumphant after these sad occasions. She forgot her nerves and raced down Regent Street, across the cobbles of the marketplace, along Trinity College Lane. As her bicycle flew over Magdalene Bridge towards her room in the house of the Archbishop's aunt, she felt her future was coming together nicely: her library post (this was before they dismissed her), 'my independence, my money, my classes' in shorthand and typing, her soapy baths at Whiters; but above all of this her closeness to Elsa.

With Elsa's encouragement, Laura had begun to relish library duties. Her job was to stack shelves, stamp books, collect fines, cover absences at the smaller satellite branches in the residential districts of Cambridge, and run errands such as bringing fresh change for the cash register. If she passed her library exams her future would be secure: she'd be able to get a job in any library, public or private – 'my lovely post, my career as librarian'.

Then came that first catastrophe. Laura was sacked.

Howl! Desolation!

It was impossible for Laura to understand why she had lost her job. The head librarian sat her down in the staff room and, just as Elsa had warned, said she was too 'dreamy', too 'muddle-headed' and 'cotton-woolish'.

Laura was certainly too cotton-woolish to comprehend what that kind of explanation meant. For the rest of her life she never understood it. Looking back when she was old, she marvelled about why she kept getting the sack from jobs during these early years. But anyone who reads the diaries can understand. Her disastrous performance as a housekeeper in the Wirral was not out of character. She was arrogant, full of cringing doubts, lazy, easily distracted and always going to the toilet.

The entries from this time raise the interesting idea that, although Laura wrote the diaries, she didn't read them. She filled the pages with words but didn't know what the words said.

On hearing about her failure at the library, Elsa revealed the full depth of her venomousness:

> E said it incredible to her that I've spoilt it all.
> E said she doesn't have such people as me for her friends.
> E said she's glad she's not my parents, to have such a child.
> E asked (moving a little from me) 'Are you insane?'

But E, even savage E, steadied her. However brutal the old woman had been to the girl, Laura could not stop herself from going back for more. Over the next days Laura knocked and knocked and knocked and knocked on Elsa's apartment door for half an hour, then sank 'weeping copious tears on the doorstep'.

Elsa would not answer the door, 'though she <u>was</u> in'.

> FOUL, BLOODY LIFE, it stinks. It is dog muck on iron-grey, ice-hard, barren pavements, and vile, noisy machines, and 'factory hand wanted, female', and ice on waste-buckets.

# 26  For years, Flora has been telling me . . .

> How I wish I was Barbara Windsor – not myself.
> She had all the attributes I would have liked,
> such as not being shy; and being a small person.
>
> **Aged fifty-five**

For years, Flora has been telling me to put Laura's books into chronological order. It maddens her to listen to me puzzle about Laura, yet still not take this basic step of sticking labels to the spines with the date written on and arranging the books in the right sequence.

I don't like the idea.

I insist that the disorder of the books captures something about Laura that the five million words written across fifteen thousand pages misses – although I'm not sure what that something is. My latest interpretation of the purpose of these books is that Laura's not writing to record her existence, she's writing to protect her brain. Her themes aren't repetitive because she keeps forgetting that she's already made the same point fifteen times before, in the same book, using exactly the same sentences, but because she's trying, by repeatedly beating the words against the page, to kill off her loneliness, her insomnia, her mother, Peter's toilet habits, her mortification that she's wasted every single one of her childhood talents, the fact that no one loves her or is willing to be loved by her, and the terrifying price of fish fillets. She's not thinking these subjects through, she's trying to knock them out. She spends so much time attempting to eliminate wretched thoughts that it's eliminating her life. As a young woman she was a good writer, but diary entries about not exploiting her talent gobbled up the time she had to develop her talent. Writing destroyed her writing.

*Feel I must write, to get things out of my System, & it takes time*

Feel I <u>must</u> must write, to get things
out of my system, & it takes time

It got in the way of piano practice and drawing exercises – the other things she was good at. Instead of preparing for her secretarial exams, paying attention during work at Cambridge Central Library, cleaning up properly for the Ellises on Wirral Point, improving her life-painting at Luton, she wrote her diary, and wondered in them why she had failed at work and art.

The result of this, I declare to Flora, is that the words in the diaries (especially the later ones) often have a dead feeling, and it's the circumstantial/incidental/conjectural things about these books that suggest life – things such as the fact that (1) at the bottom of the Ribena crate there are the decayed remains of a plastic bag, and the decay is not due to rat nibbles; (2) the lurid colour of the later volumes and the grey mood of the writing suggest a split personality; (3) Laura clearly did not read what she wrote, or did not understand what her words meant, because despite fifty years of labour she did not grasp the essential message of these pages, which any other reader spots at the first glance: namely, that her life was a failure because she never focused on anything in particular. She didn't know how to concentrate her attention. She thought of sixty ambitions:

Want to make my life a work of art

and developed none.

I want 'God' hung, drawn and quartered for how I was cheated.

It is funny that Laura gave the lamb roast to the dog when she had her disastrous post in the Wirral; it is unfathomable that she continued to throw out the best things for the rest of her life while always managing to reveal to the reader the idiocy of what she was doing, but not understanding the revelation herself.

These circumstantial/incidental/conjectural things, such as the jumble of the books, force us out of Laura's brain, back into the living world, and let us think about Laura as somebody we've just passed in the street.

It's not just Laura. The diaries teach us that it is too much to be inside anybody's head. It is a horrible place. All that repetition; that endless analysis that doesn't analyse, just mulls a point over and over until it drops dead from banality. What goes on in a person's brain is the opposite of what makes a story live. I thought Laura wrote these diaries because it confirmed that she was alive. But a lot of the time it's not 'I am alive' that she's repeating, it's 'Here I am, still sufficiently alive to try to wear down another obstacle to my contentment; here I am, still sufficiently alive to try to wear down another obstacle to my contentment; here I am, still sufficiently alive to try to . . .'

In particle physics, I suggest to Flora, beginning to sound pompous even to myself, there are two incompatible ways to describe the state of an object. The world is either captured in a slice, like a photograph, telling you with perfect accuracy where everything is, but not where it's going next; or the world is wind: nothing is visible, everything is breezes, we haven't the faintest clue where anything is, but know exactly how fast it's going and in what direction. To get round this peculiar situation, physicists have to make compromises – settle for a description of the world that is, say, two parts breezes to one part photograph.

With Laura, the disorder of the books and the plastic bag remnants are the breezes. Her words, especially by the 1990s, are the lifeless photographs.

Flora listens patiently to this agonising, waits a few more months, then makes her point again: who am I to talk in this presumptuous way? Where is my evidence for all these fancy-sounding conclusions? Have I read all the diaries? No. Have I read above a third of them? No. So, I haven't studied them properly. Do I then have any right, until I have done these basic things, to draw any conclusions about Laura whatsoever? No.

Unless I arrange the books chronologically I cannot know how everything ties together, and therefore cannot make a proper biographical study of the contents.

This morning I began to do as she said.

It has taken me until twenty past midnight. Many of the later books are, as I've explained, not dated. Laura simply arrives on page one in the middle of a Wednesday in June and bores through and out the back cover on a Friday in August. The only thing to do is read the tiny handwriting until you hit a TV celebrity death or a fresh court appearance by Michael Barrymore, then cross-check on the internet. The prawn-cocktail-pink volume is from the year 2000, because there was the unexpected news at one o'clock that John Gielgud has died; and I feel astonished that it should happen on my birthday. It is indeed a coincidence, as there were 364 other days that he could have died.

The Kool-Aid purple volume is 1996, because Laura is worried that Michael Barrymore doesn't visit his mum enough. She turned eighty-one that year. The chip-shop-mushy-pea volume is 2001, because Laura gets a hotel guide out of the library to look up the resort where Michael Barrymore is staying after 'a youth' was found floating, dead, bottom up, in his swimming pool.

Now it is done. The books are lined up in correct order on my study shelf.

And, exactly as Flora suspected, I have discovered two new facts about Laura.

The first is that my 148 diaries represent only about one eighth of the total number of volumes Laura wrote. It turns out that I don't have a single complete year after 1962, and that almost all the 70s, the second half of both the 60s and 80s, and most of the 90s are missing. From 1952, when Elsa first appeared in Laura's life, to 1958, I have nothing at all, except that one opening book of doodles. Before 1952, nothing. Estimating from these gaps in my collection, the correct total number of books is closer to a thousand, or forty million words.

The second fact: Laura is still alive.

# PART TWO

## *Crisis*

## 27 The End of history

I have a different 'God'.

**Aged sixty-two**

'Here comes the man who is going to destroy history!' declared Professor Goldthwaite, his arms aloft as I entered the room.

It was ten days after I'd discovered Laura was alive. I had come to meet Flora in a Lebanese restaurant off the Edgware Road. Waiters hurried up and down the kitchen stairs, pressing past one another along a narrow corridor, balancing plates juicy with food. Plump customers leaned against the cash desk, putting on their cashmere coats, getting ready to pay, while new arrivals, thinner and watchful, squeezed between the tables hunting for places to sit down. The air was sharp with the scent of fresh herbs and the noise of clanging colanders.

I shook the rain out of my hair and stamped my boots. I had no idea what Professor Goldthwaite was talking about. Who was this man who was going to destroy history? Why was he standing in my direction? My glasses steamed up and he and his bow tie disappeared into foggy speckles.

Professor Richard Goldthwaite is a historian from Johns Hopkins University. His *The Economy of Renaissance Florence* is 'magisterial' (*The Economist*), 'will set the parameters of the field for decades' (*Journal of Modern History*), is 'one of the most important books in Renaissance history' (*Renaissance Quarterly*).

Had he intended his announcement to refer to me? 'The destroyer of history'? How had I managed that? I can barely remember the date of Waterloo. I stepped across the room flushed with delight.

As well as Flora, there were two other academics at the table: Gian Mario, a philosopher, and Iain Fenlon, a musicologist. Iain smiled grimly at me, half stood and held out a bear-sized hand which I shook with care. He had recently saved a woman from being run over by a Post Office van by throwing himself in front of the runaway vehicle and knocking her out of the way. The woman is fine, but his back is ruined.

Gian Mario gave an amused nod. He is a specialist in scepticism, internationally renowned for the depth and meticulousness of his scholarship, and has a beard that scoops below his chin like a tooth bandage. 'Ciao,' he murmured.

'Flora's told us about your breakthrough with the diaries,' said Richard, sitting down with the careful air of an after-dinner speaker. 'Now, don't speak. Before you say anything more about it, answer this: have you written it all down? The original discovery of the books in the dumpster? The development of your theories about the author? This latest development? I mean *everything*. Everything you have thought about this . . . person.' He said the last word quizzically, as though there might still be some doubt that Laura had stopped being merely a noun and become flesh and blood. '*Everything* you've conjectured. It is very important for the future of my subject that you answer this question carefully. Thousands of livelihoods may depend upon it.'

'Of course.' I felt a stir of self-confidence, because I could answer the question so easily. 'I write everything down as I go along. Why?'

'And when you made your breakthrough, you had already done this writing? You didn't do it after the scoop? It's very important to be clear about that.'

'All written before. I've been working on these diaries for four years, and only discovered that she was alive last week.'

'You understand my point? You've found documents about a person, studied them believing the person to be dead, formed your opinions about who the person was, what she was like, why she did the things she did, and now you've discovered she's alive. Imagine if the subject of my recent book, Jacopo Peri, the man who wrote the first opera, suddenly walked through that door, able to challenge everything I have conjectured. Thank God, that will never happen, because he died four hundred years ago. My conjectures will never be called into question by the only person who knows the truth. But for the first time in historical research, you have written a portrait of a dead person, and then the dead person has come to life! It could be a catastrophe for historical research. What if all our ideas about how to interpret documents are wrong? That is why it is so important to know: have you written all your thoughts down – all the ones you had *before* you knew she was alive – and definitely not touched it? Think carefully: the future of history hangs in the balance . . .'

'Not touched it since. Not a word,' I confirmed, beginning to think rather highly of myself.

Richard sighed with satisfaction and picked up a menu. 'Everything that I have worked for in the last fifty years depends on the truth of that answer.'

'All I have to do now is get Laura's permission to publish everything I've written, and I can send the manuscript to the publishers to see if they'll buy it.'

Richard slapped his menu back down on the table. 'You mean you haven't sent your manuscript in yet?'

'No. I need to meet Laura first, then I . . .'

'So you could still have tampered with it in the days since your discovery?'

'Well, I suppose . . .'

'Phew!' interrupted Richard, falling back in his chair and making a melodramatic gesture across his brow. 'History is saved.'

Before I discovered that she was alive, I'd known that Laura was dead. In the British Library, against my better judgement and despite Vince the detective's suggestion, I'd checked in the register of deaths and been lucky again. I hadn't found anyone suitable in Cambridge named Laura born in 1939, but that didn't mean she was alive. I couldn't find her in the register of births either, and that didn't make her not exist. After gazing at the microfiches for ten minutes I'd got bored. I don't like this kind of research. It reminds me of the worst school mathematics, repetitious and inching along. Laura was dead, that's what mattered. I'd decided on a likely sequence of events: Laura had died two years before Peter, which was why the books had been thrown out. Peter must have stashed the diaries in a cupboard. When he died, in came the house-clearance people, and bang! everything was chucked out.

Why had I decided she'd died two years earlier? I'm not sure. It popped up as a guess one day and then, as tidy narratives do, it became the truth. Two years felt about right. Deaths should not occur too close together.

'It was because Flora told me to put the diaries in chrono-logical order that I realised Laura was still alive,' I explained to Richard. 'I found that the last diary I had was from August 2001 – just weeks before my friend tipped herself into the skip. Instead of Peter outlasting Laura, I opened this volume to discover Laura sitting at the kitchen table thinking about Peter's ashes, after his cremation.'

It was early evening. The brown light of the declining day had stretched across the rolled-up carpet and thrown itself into the kitchen chairs. Laura sat at the table, not paying attention. The crockery and all but the essential pots and pans had been taken away. The paintings in the corridor had gone. 'Now' – the only moment that ever matters to Laura – had brought her to the end of fifty years. 'Now' she had been a fourteen-year-old girl weeping tears of love at her piano for her teacher. 'Now' she had been an artist in London, burning to take on the world, eager to suffer for beauty and truth. 'Now' she had become a housekeeper, but soon she would be a concert pianist. Now she was here, alone, middle-aged, sitting at a wooden table listening to the creaks and ticks of a house that didn't belong to her. She felt that she had always been going to be here. This 'now' was the same 'now' she had been thinking of half a century ago, when she'd stood on the ridge of Whitefield among the 'sprinkled oats' and wondered what would become of her in the 'fever and fret of modern life'.

Peter's house was in a disgraceful state. Cupboard doors were open, shelves emptied, dust that was a century old exposed. There were fresh splinters of wood at the edge of the floor. A few months before he died, Peter had whispered to his friend Lynley that he had twenty-five secret 'cubby holes' around the house in which he had stashed jewels and millions of pounds' worth of postage stamps. He wanted Lynley to have them; he had drawn a map of the house to reveal where these hiding places were, so that Lynley could extract them before the house was sold. But he had also hidden the map, and before he could tell Lynley where it was, Peter had had a stroke.

Even before the body was burned, Lynley and another of Peter's friends, Tom, had started coming round twice a week to tap their knuckles against the wainscot, yank at floorboards and shuffle about in the attic poking through boxes. They unscrewed the legs of Peter's bed, opened up the mattress, upended the tea caddy in the larder (although 'there were finger marks in the dust, so if there had been anything in it, the assessors have got there first'), peered through the ventilation bricks at the base of the house, lowered a torch tied to a piece of string into a cavity discovered under the sitting room, and picked back the lino in the upstairs 'slouch' (Laura's word for a toilet). Among the things they found were a copy of the *Daily Telegraph* dated 1971 and an old French shopping list, which Lynley scuttled off to have evaluated. It was worth 75p. Lynley decided to bring in 'a medium in Teddington called "Brenda", who specialised in 'finding things'. He showed her pictures of the stamps and offered her £75 for an afternoon of psychic concentration.

She saw no Penny Blacks.

Laura helped Lynley and Tom conduct these ravenous searches, but she wasn't greedy herself. The moment a new 'hotspot for a cubby hole' occurred to her, she rang up Lynley to let him know, and then prepared lunch or tea while he prised away the panels and levered up floorboards.

> I haven't enjoyed such kindness from people since 1993 – and it has made all the difference, after Peter's death; the nuisance of people coming, and being the society hostess, small price to pay.

When Peter's will was read, it turned out that he had excluded Lynley. It's hard not to suspect that all that talk of 'cubby holes' somewhere 'in the structure of the house' had been a dying man's practical joke on a rapacious friend. Whispering to Lynley just before his fatal stroke that there was a treasure map, but that it was also hidden in one of the unfindable 'cubby holes', is a delightfully mischievous touch.

With an oddly contrasting lack of imagination, Peter left the house to St John's College, one of the richest in the country. It quickly hawked the property to a developer, and the lawyers wanted Laura out of the house asap. She had no money. She had lived there for thirty years, half her life. Everybody she had loved had died while she'd been cocooned in this building. She was to be evicted by the end of the week.

She clung on for six months.

'Of course, all my own plans in my youth were just a pie in the sky,' Laura writes on the closing page of the final entry of the last book, 'as I have a different "God".'

The next morning, as I picture things, the clearance men swarmed in and pitched Laura on the street. In the confusion, she left behind 148 of her diaries; the men dumped those in the skip from which Dido rescued them later that afternoon.

After that the developer sliced open the front hedge, rammed a tarmac drive up its rose bower and built two Arts and Crafts mock-ups on the old pear orchard. One of the most lovely and private houses in Cambridge was turned into an advert from *Suburban Fantasy Home Monthly*.

'Once I realised that Laura might still be alive,' I continued with my explanation to Richard, 'I made quick progress. For £9.50 I checked the online electoral register, and discovered her last name. Ten minutes later I was looking into her living room on Google Earth.'

It had taken me a while to get used to the Google controls. Each time I came close to where Laura's new house should be, the orientation buttons became wildly sensitive, shot me past as if I'd slipped on a patch of oil and repositioned me thirty-five miles above Scotland.

Eventually I'd mastered my excitement. Laura Francis's semi-detached bungalow is at the end of a short cul-de-sac on a developer's estate. It squats beside the pavement like a resting fly. The front wall faces the road, and has a glazed door and side panel. Pieces of post have climbed up the glass below the letter-box. They are still there as I correct this final draft of the manuscript.

In front of the house is a miniature front garden with fuchsias and evergreen shrubs bordering a patch of mildly overgrown grass; a dingy, run-down scene. A narrow drive runs up to the side of the bungalow, squashes past a fence, passes a door and ends at a wooden garage. A small collection of cooking implements and food tins is piled next to the door, which is slightly ajar, as though Laura is on the other side, enjoying the first catch of the morning breeze.

The Lebanese food arrived, steaming and fat. The conversation with Richard, Gian Mario, Iain and Flora changed. It wasn't until the end of the meal that I remembered I had brought one of Laura's books with me to read on the tube, and fetched it from my raincoat. It was from 1978 – the Middle Period of Laura's life, when all the volumes are the same: small, hard-backed, dark red, with the word 'IDEAL' impressed in gold outline letters down the spine. 1978 is one of the few almost complete years in the collection. Elsa is dead. Elsa's temporary rival Dame Harriette is dead. All talk of becoming a writer or artist has stopped. The handwriting has begun to shrink, but Laura is still following the printed lines on the page. She has been working for Peter for four years, and has realised again that she might be a musical genius.

> The exquisite, simple little minuet in the Haydn sonata makes me weep this morning. I play it so expressively, know that I really am musical. Even on the radio, a pianist may not play it with such sensitivity and personal feeling as I do.

Once more, the reader sees immediately what Laura does not: that she has forgotten to consider the only important element in any judgement about her musicality, i.e. a listener who is not herself. Her reason for believing she is a great musician is because she is playing for herself only, to herself only. She is deafened by solipsism.

Richard wiped his hands, took the book and held it up with teasing solemnity, like a libation. He didn't look inside. Richard never looks at anything immediately. After a second he offered the parcel across to Iain, who carefully turned it over and back and over again: back cover, front cover, top and bottom of spine. He made appreciative smacking noises between his teeth and treated the volume as though it were a small anaesthetised animal.

'It reminds me of that very sad story about Frank Kermode . . .'

'Precisely,' I interrupted. 'That's exactly what my friend Dido said when she took the books out of the skip.'

'Hhhhhh*rrrrrrrrrumm*mmph!' Iain cleared his throat. 'I know because I was with Frank on the day it happened. He came to college for supper that evening, directly afterwards. He was in shock. He was completely dazed. He chewed his pipe and said, in his characteristically understated way, "I've had a bit of a problem." That afternoon, two chaps in high-vis jackets had arrived at the door of his house to move his books to his new flat, and Frank had said, "Come in, come in." Now, in many circles Frank was regarded as the greatest living critic of certain types of English literature, and he died when he was ninety, so he had lived a very long time – he had a lot of signed first editions.'

But the two men weren't the removal men, they were the city refuse collectors, and it wasn't until they'd taken out quite a few of the boxes that Kermode realised they were throwing them in the crusher.

'For the rest of his life,' said Iain, his voice catching with the awfulness of this story, 'Frank's library began with the letter I, because A to H had been pulped.'

Iain took a deep breath, let out the air meditatively and handed the book to Gian Mario.

Gian Mario inclined his long Roman face forward, gave the book two barely perceptible nods of appreciation, then returned his gaze to mid-air. Stillness and Gian Mario have an opaque relationship. His gesture could mean that he thought nothing of Laura and the diaries, or that he thought everything of them, and was now imagining what a project this would be in the hands of a true scholar.

'There must be in mythology or philosophy somewhere,' I suggested, 'a figure who represents what she is – a figure of failure on all fronts. A stock character who stands for the fear of becoming Laura Francis: the person who ends up not meeting a single one of her hopes and gets thrown out in a skip. That's why this is a valuable life. She can be an excellent writer, she is a good artist, perhaps she had the makings of a pianist too, but the real thing is that Laura Francis represents in a pure form the feeling that everyone feels, of a life not lived.'

Gian Mario cosseted his beard, stared at his fruit salad, then nodded. 'Do you know her state of mind now? No? Do you think she is sad?'

'I've written to her twice. The first time I said I was a biographer and I was researching a book that I thought she could help me with. I began that one, "Are you the Laura Francis who used to work for Professor Peter Mitchell?" I didn't say anything about the diaries. I didn't want to horrify her! I just said, "I'm a biographer, and if I've got the right Laura Francis could we meet?" '

'And?'

'She didn't reply.'

'Sensible woman. How do you know she received this letter?'

'I sent it recorded delivery, and then checked the tracking number online. She signed for it.' Seeing this record of her signature, just a tick in a box on the Royal Mail website, had been the first real sign I'd had that Laura was not just alive, but moving, conscious, more than a piece of government data. That tick had been a clod of earth kicked off her grave. 'Last week I sent another letter. But this time I tried a different tactic. I said, "Next Thursday I will be in Auntie's Tea Shop in Cambridge at 4 o'clock." '

'Auntie's Tea Shop?'

'I know she knows it. It's got lace and cakes under glass. "Come and meet me," I said. "If you like, please bring a friend." I didn't want her to feel nervous, she's seventy-three years old, and a very fearful sort of woman.'

'And rightly so, with people like you around! Poor woman,' said Richard. 'I think we should warn her – There's a biographer on the loose. He knows where you live.'

'Then I said, "If you don't show up at 4 o'clock, I will come and knock on your door at 5.30. And I will also be in Auntie's Tea Shop on Friday at 4 o'clock. If you can't make that appointment either, I will come up to your house at 5.30 that day, too." '

'That's harassment.'

'Nonsense. If she really doesn't want to see me, all she's got to do is not show up twice and hide in her bathroom twice. I've given her four ways to say no, so I can be perfectly clear that's what she really wants, and won't spend the rest of my life wondering if her lack of reply is simply due to the fact that she lost my first letter with the return address, or that it wasn't actually her who signed for it, or that I missed her by ten minutes because just before my letters came she was taken off to a home.'

'What do you think will be her attitude to this book,' pursued Gian Mario in a pleasant and remorseless way, 'in which you are going to reveal everything about this sensitive, frightened woman?'

'I should think she'll run a mile.'

'Do you think she might be right to have the police waiting for you?'

Richard reached across to where Gian Mario had placed the diary, and took it back. He laid it down on the table, lifted the taut, red cover with one hand and, as if moving bubbles across the surface of water, flattened back the opening page with the other.

'So you carry this about in your pocket? The End of History – like a bag of potato chips?'

# 28 Auntie's Tea Shop is a seaside shop . . .

Oh, glorious blaze of the imaginative world!
Would like to enter into it again and write, write, write;
only stopping for meals or a walk, as I used to.
A pity that I can not allow myself to do that now –
the material business of everyday life has to be seen to.
I have nothing to say.

**Aged twenty-five**

Auntie's Tea Shop is a seaside shop fifty miles from the coast. It is just off the market square, in the middle of Cambridge. Squashed between the university outfitters and a shop selling nasty key fobs with scorpions trapped inside, it's a place for under-graduates to bring their bored parents after a tour of the colleges.

Dido and I arrived an hour early. Doctors, especially when they have not been ill themselves, make a great point about not letting their patients give in to desperation. But behind the sensible advice and encouraging expressions, their drugs are also desperation. Dido was exhausted from her latest round of chemotherapy. The tumours weren't responding. She'd lost two stone. It was difficult to tell which was murdering her quicker: nature or medicine.

She sat down and disappeared behind a pile of Thomas More papers. I kept my eye on the other customers. There were two elderly ladies and a large young man with a pony-tail. The man's knees bumped about under his table, making the crockery rattle. One of the women looked up sharply.

She was tall, in her early seventies and busty. She wore thin-rimmed glasses. Immediately I caught her eye she stood up, reached into her trouser pocket and, staring back at me, pulled out something white and crumpled as if it had been scrunched up in a rage.

It was a handkerchief.

She dabbed her mouth and caught the waitress's eye.

'*Die Rechnung, bitte, Hannah. Danke sehr.*'

The waitress answered, also in German, and brought a small docket with a sweet rolling on top of it.

Dido looked at me, shook her head and went back to work.

Once this customer had gone, a silence settled on the room, pinned into place by the occasional clink of the sugar tongs and then, half a minute later, by an unguarded slurp. The second woman in the room was short, flat-chested, and wasn't wearing glasses to read the *Telegraph*.

> There is absolutely nothing in the papers; and Peter's paper [the *Telegraph*] just a load of rubbish, absolutely worthless – one could get a lot of cans of drink, for the money.

I ordered a toasted tea-cake and settled down. I had thought carefully about which diary to bring with me. A volume from the 1960s, when Laura was on the toilet half the time? The 1970s, when she was overwhelmed by her love for ninety-nine-year-old Dame Harriette? The 1980s, after E's death, when, disorientated and alone, she contemplates suicide? The 1990s, when she is possibly mad? Any one of them might make her lunge at me. I'd chosen one from 1959:

> am so on fire with inspiration at the day, deep, deep feeling of magic and a frenzy of enthusiasm & exaltation, as if I would burst. Really lived today, wide

awake, observing people and things. Practically swore to my sisters I'd BE A WRITER.

It was the tail end of the only time she was truly happy. So many 'happy memories;– of laughter & health & passionate, crazy love'. She was living in Cambridge in 'the fugitive bliss' of Miss Ramsey's house on Castle Hill, visiting Whiters and E regularly, and working on her third novel about John Gielgud, which she called 'the histoire':

> After tea, finished chapter of histoire. Mozart piano was on (K.333) whilst I wrote a little c-feel when Val has met John in the park. C. feels physically so exciting – sent my heart beating at a terrific rate, really uncomfortable, until I have written it down & the discomfort subsides, & I feel happy and elated.

Staring at the second woman in the tea room, it occurred to me that I didn't know the first thing about Laura Francis. Why couldn't this petite lady with good eyesight and worried politics be the tall, myopic, 42B, embittered *Sun* reader of the diaries? There was nothing illogical about that. The petite woman might have written herself as Laura Francis precisely because she was not Laura Francis. The diaries were a way for her to let her inner Laura Francis exist – the equivalent of a stockbroker wearing his mini-skirts in the attic. All the best biographical subjects are like this to some degree. Just when you've got them trussed up in your biographical turkey pan, they do something unexpected, offhand – such as turning out to have no sense of causality (my first subject, the homeless Stuart), or anecdote (my second, the mathematical prodigy Simon), or rising, Christ-like, from the dead – and you realise that you're as far away from success as you ever were. You're back to scrabbling around the turkey yard.

There is something very appealing about this constant failure of biography: you set out to capture; you think for a second that you have, and have therefore made the world of interesting characters a slightly tidier place; and then you discover you've made a mess of the job – and it is a relief. You are less destructive because your tidying has been unsuccessful.

Perhaps this woman reading the newspaper had come along to today's meeting knowing that I would never suspect her, so that she could get a good look at me and assess what was her best next move. Perhaps the young man was part of an insightful experiment devised by the department of sociology to publicise a forged diary, released into the world via the 'skip method'. As soon as one allowed for any unravelling in the truthfulness of Laura Francis, there was nothing to stop her entire story falling to pieces. All I had to rely on was the assumption that when people wrote they were Laura Francis, they meant it.

Without a glance in my direction, the second woman got up and left.

Three Japanese women came in and sat down in a sigh of giggles. An old man, sunk inside a jacket that had been sewn on when he was young and massive, settled by jolts next to the cake stand.

When I had first used my computer to creep up to Laura's bungalow, 150 miles away, I was shocked to find her standing behind the window staring back at me: a freakishly outsized woman in an off-white, almost grey toga. She was watching the Google camera car go by as it filmed her house.

She had her head chopped off.

It was only when I recovered my nerve and got closer that I realised it was her curtains, not her, in the window. They had fallen off the rail in a way that resembled clothing. What I had thought was her decapitated neck was the top of the window frame.

At 4.37, seven minutes late, the door chimes jangled and I started up from my daydream, grabbing for my digital voice recorder. A glint of light reflected by the door glass dazzled me, and for a second I saw the headless giantess again, stepping towards me. Then the angle of reflection changed and reality came back.

It was the boy with the ponytail going out.


I know Hugh, the second-hand-bookstall man in the market square; he's there every Tuesday and Thursday. As Dido and I walked away from Auntie's, we stopped to speak to him – during the 1990s Laura repeatedly mentions buying books from Hugh. It seemed obvious that he would immediately know who I was talking about: the tall woman with glasses who bought, let's see, a book about Rose West twelve years ago. It would have been Hugh's Tuesday stand, because it was a paperback.

'Not just that, of course – lots of books,' I added. 'She's very tall. Hair reddy-brown, or would have been reddy-brown when she was younger. Oh, I know! She also bought an Enid Blyton children's book in 1979. Were you here in 1979?'

I showed him the diary from 1959. 'She had handwriting like this.'

Hugh is an amiable but busy man. He shuffled the hardback he was carrying into a packing box, smiled and moved along the trestle table.


Dido was too tired to go on, and sagged off home. It was better for me to appear at Laura's house on my own. Dido and

Richard had found her, but I was the one who'd spent five years thinking of her as a friend.

I arrived at her estate with ten minutes to spare. It is a large place, with coiling streets and unfenced front gardens that give it an American bonhomie. Contented suburban noises drifted through the summer air after the morning rain, the edges plucked off by the surrounding roofs and trees: somebody strimming grass with what sounded like a large bee; children playing football, but no sounds of the kicks or a ball; a radio playing swing music, mingled with the sweet smell of a barbecue; the soft tink! tink! tink! of a hammer mending a piece of metallic machinery. Several of the bungalows at the start of Laura's road had their garage doors open, with shining cars inside and tools hanging obediently from hooks along one wall – but there was no one visible. It was a safe, self-confident street.

At 5.29 I gripped my voice recorder in the palm of my hand with my finger over the record button and began the walk to the bungalow.

Laura's semi-detached bungalow was towards the end of the cul-de-sac, and exactly as Google had pictured it: tight and grubby. The side door was still ajar, with several empty tins of cat food scattered outside as well as a saucepan, a pink fake-crystal vase, and a paperweight in the shape of an owl. Through an adjoining window I could make out a small kitchen. The overhead grill on the gas stove had a thin grey blanket resting over it; by squinting my eyes I could see that it was a swag of cobwebs and dust. Tins, books, egg cartons, ready-meal packs, a frying pan, boxes and plates were piled on top of the sink and the sideboard to a height of three feet – and the cobweb blanket had leaped across and swarmed over this too, as far as the opposite wall.

Leaves and plastic packaging rustled about my feet.

The subject of my previous book had been a messy person too. I felt disappointed. I didn't want to have to use the same imagery again.

I heard a man's voice from the neighbouring house, and turning round saw a friendly, round face staring back at me from the door of his bungalow, which also led into his kitchen.

'Is this Laura Francis's house?' I called. 'Do you know where she's gone? I wrote her a letter, I've come to do an interview . . .'

'Yes, mate. Laura Francis? Of course I know where she is. Everybody round here knows Laura Francis.'

'Can you tell me where she is?'

'Where she is?' the man looked amused. 'Don't you know?'

'No, I've never met her before, I've just . . .'

'She's standing behind you.'

# 29 Hello! Are you Laura Francis?

Transcribed, with some editing and additions
for clarity, from the digital voice recorder
I'd hidden in my jacket pocket.

*Hello! Are you Laura Francis?*

Are you Alex?

*Hello! Hello!*

Hello! You know, I was just thinking about you. I feel I've
been very impolite not to reply to your card. I've been living
with my mother.

*Ahhhhhh, right, right.*

Yes, yes.

*Um . . .?*

Well!

*Do you mind if I come in, or . . .?*

Yes, ah, I'm afraid the place is in a terrible state.

*That's all right. I'm used . . . I don't mind . . . oh!*

Well, Alex, um, okay, well . . .

> (A NOTE on her voice: It is, during greetings
> and polite small talk, high-pitched, often
> rising in the middle or at the end of sentences,
> as if she is talking kindly to a cat. When she
> is talking to a cat (she looks after two) it is
> higher still. As conversation progresses, it gets
> deeper.)

*Um, where shall I sit?*

Why don't you sit here?

*But that doesn't leave you any place to sit.*

Oh, it doesn't matter.

*Where are you going to sit?*

I'll sit here.

*Where should I put this?*

There.

*And this?*

There. I think I'm one of these hoarders.

*I think you are, yes.*

I find things at charity shops.

*But you're not as bad as some of them.*

Yes, yes.

*There was one the other night, wasn't there? His went right up to the ceiling.*

Oh, that man with the newspapers. BBC2.

*And he crawled along. You know how he crawled along! You've got a few feet left before you match him.*

Yes, ha, ha, yes.

*He was magnificent.*

He was an intelligent man.

*So, um, gosh, so this is your, um, this is your bungalow.*

Yes, Alex, that's right.

*That's right. So, let's see, how do I begin? Do you have any idea why I'm here?*

No.

*Well, it's a . . . it's a very odd story, this. I don't quite know how to begin. Okay, what happened is, a friend of mine – this was about 2001 – was just, came across this skip, and I don't know if you know, or how it happened, but a load of your diaries were thrown in the skip.*

Oh yes.

*Did you know about this?*

No, I didn't actually.

*Well, there were quite a lot of them, and I wanted to find out who I should return them to. Anyway, I had to look through. I didn't read very much at all. And I assumed you were dead. And I looked at them to try to find out who you were because you hadn't put your name on, and I thought this is quite intriguing, but I wonder who this person is. I didn't read very much . . . but while I was looking to find out how to get the books back to you or your heirs I thought this would be an interesting subject for a book . . .*

Oh, hmm, heh, heh, aaah . . .

*And then when I discovered you were alive, I thought I'd better come and speak to you and wondered whether this was even conceivable as a possibility. I know it comes . . . I don't know quite how to say . . . it's such a weird thing to bring up. But as a result of this friend of mine finding all these books thrown out, I thought . . . a book based on your private diaries.*

I'd cooperate in anything you wanted to know, yes.

*Gosh!*

Yes, I'm just on one at the moment actually. I was writing about you. Now let me see. Here it is. 'I'd intended to go to the bank this afternoon, written the cheque. But I am gnashing' – you know, because it was raining. 'So I just had four walls instead. It isn't even a shower, just going on and on, so I thought I'd sort out the mail. Thought I'd have the opportunity. As I expected, that Masters man has not given up. But he sent a card and said he'll be at Auntie's tea rooms on Tuesday or Friday, but unfortunately he hasn't put a date on the card. It could be a fortnight ago or it could be tomorrow. I don't really like people coming to the house because it's in such a state. I expect he's been to see the bungalow because he seems so interested. If he has a car, which I've no doubt he has, he almost certainly has been and he may even have seen me for all I know'.

*How extraordinary! How extraordinary though, how
extraordinary. So in principle it's not a thing you'd object to?
One thing I didn't expect was that you would be so unflustered,
take it utterly in your stride, I'd thought, gosh, I'm going to have
to approach this very, very delicately.*

No.

During this first interview, Laura showed me a collection
of drawings she'd done as an art student at Camberwell,
aged twenty-three. This one is a self-portrait.

*I'd add to that, that I would not want to publish anything you hadn't seen. I'd want to do it with your cooperation.*

I've really done very little. It's all been a disappointment, my life, yes . . .

*Would you say your diaries represent you?*

Well I think so, yes.

*I know people who write diaries and they only write them when they're furious and they're not by nature furious people.*

I think some of the things I put in my diaries were really cruel actually, really bitter.

*Yes, some of them.*

Yes, uncensored.

*To me as a biographer it's a goldmine. Someone writing without any attempt to hide their thoughts.*

I didn't want to deceive anybody. I just put what I really thought.

*It doesn't bother you that I've read that, and . . .*

No, it doesn't bother me. There's no point in writing it down if nobody ever reads it.

*But you weren't writing for anyone?*

Oh no, I was doing it for myself.

*How much time do you spend writing?*

An hour and a half a day?

*What happens when you finish one?*

It just sits around.

*So when you finish a diary do you look back to it?*

No, just go on to the next one.

*You didn't throw them out yourself, did you?*

No, certainly not!

*But you had no sense of these diaries having gone missing?*

There have been so many. They've all really rather gone astray.

*Where are your other diaries? You must have written thousands. Someone who can lose their diaries with such ease as you can seems to have the wrong spirit for a hoarder.*

Well, hehe, hehe, hmmmm … I don't really know what's happened to them. There might be some in the garage.

*You're not worried about them?*

Well, it's not much use worrying about them, if they've gone.

*But don't you want to preserve what you write?*

It's more of a compulsion really. I just enjoy writing. I enjoy the sound of the words. I've done it since I was about twelve. I just like the feeling of the pen on the page.

*And if one day you stopped doing it, what would you feel?*

I wouldn't quite feel myself.

*Tell me about your mother.*

Ohhhhh, ooooohhhh, well, she's had a very happy life. A lot happier than mine. Went up to Cambridge, met my dad and they got married and were very happy and then came the war and my mum went to live at Whitefield.

*Tell me about Whitefield.*

I think it got burned down. Yes, it would seem I was a very lucky person. One would think I had a silver spoon in my mouth, but that just didn't happen.

*Do you play the piano still?*

I broke my wrist a few years back, and I stopped playing.

*Do you draw ever?*

No.

*Just the diaries left?*

Yes.

*In your early diaries you drew a face – always the same face, a sort of Shakespearean character . . .*

Oh, John Gielgud. Yes, I wondered where that box of books had got to. I couldn't find them when I left.

*Well, they went to me!*

Whitefield House, from the back

Yes, I was very keen on John Gielgud when I was younger. I was always drawing him.

*Page after page of John Gielgud!*

Yes. I can't bear the man now.

*What made you go off him?*

I met him at Trinity bookshop. He was signing his book and I went to say 'Hello' and he just cut me dead. Didn't want to meet me. He just looked at me as if I was somebody he didn't like.

*Do you think you're happy now?*

Happy's a bit much. I'm not miserable the way I was before.

*When did that change?*

Since I've been living here. Since I got older. You just come to terms with things. I wish I hadn't done this, I wish I hadn't done that, but there's nothing much I can do about that now.

*Does there come a point when regrets stop?*

There's not much point in regrets, is there? I've got on better here than I expected. I spend my day writing and reading. I always get three papers a day: the *Mail*, the *Mirror* and the *Express*. All the medical articles in the Tuesday papers. I want to improve my knowledge about how things are progressing. You must be a nice person if my cat puts up with you.

*If we were to do this book, do you not worry about the fact that people would read all the stuff in your diaries?*

Noooo, I don't think so, no.

*Your neighbours?*

I don't think people on the estate would be interested. They're mostly old people, on their way out. The ambulance comes up here every few days.

*As I say, you'd have the right to veto the entire project if you don't like it.*

Yes, well, that's okay, yes.

*What do you think your mother will say?*

I don't think she'll mind really.

*And your family, your sisters?*

I don't think they'll mind, yes.

*You don't always say very nice things about them.*

Oh, don't I? Noooo. Hmm.

*What do you imagine such a biography might be like, about you?*

I really don't know. Obviously it will be about someone who's been very disappointed in life, but I haven't been on drink or drugs or anything like that. It's not that degree of disaster. You know, a lot of people have been much worse off and had worse lives.

*I'd assumed this book would end with a picture of your gravestone! How do you cook? Because your stove isn't accessible. It's under that blanket of dust and those tins.*

I got my gas cut off. I had a row with the gas people. Before I lived here they charged me all the wrong bills, I just couldn't get it sorted out, they charged me as if I was living here and then in the end they cut me off.

*But that was ten years ago.*

I have this little electric. I just boil things.

*It doesn't seem very convenient.*

No, it's not the way I really want to live.

*But your fridge works?*

Yes. Also, I have a little garden at the back.

*Do you do much gardening?*

No, I hate gardening. Another bit of my story is that I fell deeply in love with a lady who was a concert pianist when I was a girl, a lady who was a refugee, had come over from Germany. I fell so

Jacket illustration by Laura Francis for a book of Italian recipes

deeply in love with her that it went on for years and years. She was far older than me, of course – there was fifty years between us. Yes, from that age I was in love with her and it didn't change.

*What was it about her?*

Well, she played the piano. She was a wonderfully gifted concert pianist. She used to play professionally when she was in Germany. She used to play for me personally – that's really quite wonderful, isn't it?

*Did anything ever happen between you?*

Oh no! She wouldn't have liked anything like that.

*You didn't mind that?*

Oh no, certainly not. I did find her attractive. A little person, a little tiny person. Yes . . . I'm not as successful as the others have been in my family. I've not got married. I've really rather felt a failure.

*It's no good if you're going to fall in love with a woman who's fifty years older.*

It's ridiculous, isn't it? It's ridiculous! I just had such strong feelings for her I didn't really bother with anybody else. It's really a bit strange, isn't it? It seems a bit strange. I think I would have liked to have got married. Didn't have much chance to meet people, we lived out in the country.

*Male or female would you like to be with?*

I think a man probably, yes, yes.

*But your sisters met people.*

Yes, they did, but they were car drivers.

*I think even a bicycle driver can meet somebody.*

Anyway, it's not an issue now.

*I wanted to ask you about one of the books – the first one I have in the collection: 1952. [I hand it to her.] Are there any particular thoughts you have about this book?*

Oh, yes, yes [laughing], yes, I vaguely remember this. I was about twelve or thirteen. This is a birthday list. 'Gun for Henry'

– Henry was a doll. Yes! These are portraits of E.

*Those horrible ones of platypus mouth are E?*

[More laughter] Yes! Yes, they're all E, it's E again and again and again.

*If you look at the back, you'll see some of the pages have been taken out, as if with a razor.*

Yes, I see.

*What's that about? It appeared to me violent and exciting.*

Perhaps my dad used the pages. We were very far from the shops.

*So there was nothing more dramatic about it at all? I had all sorts of sinister ideas about it. I thought you had severed the pages because they contained a terrible secret or* [said with hope] *perhaps E?*

Perhaps my dad needed some paper and took these ones out to draw on. He was an amateur artist and sculptor. He made figures in clay.

*Did he really? What sort of figures?*

He made a little gnome for the garden.

(For the next few minutes, Laura looked through the book, delighted, laughing frequently. I had got a lot wrong. The drawing of the ballet dancer on page 99 was not by her, but by her sister Jennifer. The faint figure weeping at the piano, of which I make heavy weather on page 102, is not a tragic image of herself, but just another picture of E, dozing on the keys.)

And this one is E, and here's another, and that one . . . She was a very funny person to look at. This drawing is by me. I remember that, ha, ha, ha! This is William. I loved the William books, ha, ha! I wasn't into sport. I read William books.

*Who's your favourite writer now?*

I like some of Iris Murdoch. I like Dickens. I'm fond of Dickens. I'm reading *Rebecca* at the moment, because that's so real.

> (An hour had passed. I got up to go. On my way out I noticed a book on top of the piano. As if put there as a joke, it was *Dusty Answer*, by Rosamond Lehmann, with an epigraph from Meredith:
>
> Ah, what a dusty answer gets the soul
>
> When hot for certainties in this our life!
>
> In the kitchen, I touched the swag of dust over the stove.)

*It's like a fabric, isn't it? It's rather wonderful.*

It is really. It's not what my family would think. They'd be horrified. Oh well, goodbye, goodbye.

*I'll ring next time I'm here, and I can begin showing you the manuscript. Is there anything in the diaries that you feel you wouldn't want discussed?*

Not really, no, because it wouldn't be true otherwise.

## 30  Epitaph

Here lies Laura Francis,
Who did nothing,
Went nowhere,
Was loved by nobody.

**Epitaph suggested by E**

'Ah, what a dusty answer gets the soul, when hot for certainties
in this our life!' The quote inside the book on Laura's piano
pestered me home. Laura had been hot for certainties: the
certainty that she was an artist; the certainty that she was
capable of writing an opera; the certainty that she was a rival to
van Gogh; the certainty that she would one day be published.

Laura had got a dusty answer. She had ended up spending
over a quarter of a century as a housekeeper-companion to a
dehydrated professor of IT – a Victorian job trapped in the
twentieth century, for which she was paid, per month, less
than the average worker was earning in a week.

I'm the most illiterate writer I've ever met. I can spend five
years studying diaries nobody wants in which nothing
happens, but I've never read the classics. When I reached
London, I found a café and looked up the lines from Meredith.
The quotation is from his novella in verse called *Modern Love*,
one of the first 'psychological' poems. I downloaded a copy
from Internet Archive. Published in 1862, it is about the
break-up of a marriage, told in fifty sonnets.

The narrator is the husband, speaking sometimes in the first
person, sometimes in the third. The man's wife (generally

assumed to be based on Meredith's first wife) has betrayed him. In gloominess he finds a mistress, but he can't love her because he still loves his wife. There is no clarity or resolution. Over fifty pages the husband and wife destroy each other. He is cold, aloof, hurt, inconsistent, disdainful. She is broken. Desperate not to expose their failure to the world, they pretend to their friends that they are happy; determined to be masterful and polite, they sleep, side by side, 'Like sculptured effigies they might be seen/upon their marriage-tomb, the sword between'.

I must have been in an odd mood, because I couldn't let these overwrought, occasionally clunky, subtle poems go. I repeatedly had to get up from my café table with my eyes smarting and a catch in my throat and try to pace off my emotion in front of the sandwich refrigerator; then I'd jump into the next sonnet so fast that I couldn't understand what Meredith was talking about. The words were made from trumpet blasts. The punctuation boomed with exclamations. Forcing myself to be calmer, I went through the sonnet a second time and saw that it was perfectly clear: the poem was about Laura.

> Cold as a mountain in its star-pitched tent,
> Stood high Philosophy, less friend than foe:
> Whom self-caged Passion, from its prison-bars,
> Is always watching with a wondering hate.

It was simply a matter of translating the terms correctly. E was self-caged Passion, enraged by her failure as an artist, taking it out on Laura. 'High Philosophy' was to be read as 'High Art' in Laura's case, 'less friend than foe'. She had watched High Art all her life with 'a wondering hate' – hatred of her inability to grasp it.

In Love's deep woods,
I dreamt of loyal Life: – The offence is there!
Love's jealous woods about the sun are curled;
At least the sun far brighter there did beam. –
My crime is, that the puppet of a dream,
I plotted to be worthy of the world.

Those last two lines are not Meredith reflecting back to when his marriage was happy; they are Laura at the edge of Whiters' wood, gazing down at Cambridge, speculating on her future life as a triumph 'in three or four different mediums', including being 'an authority and writer on Shakespeare'.

The poems were not just about Laura, they were also about Dido, now too weak to get out of bed, who was not going to finish her groundbreaking book on Thomas More or her six-hundred-page 'fiendishly devilish' murder mystery, and about Richard beating his legs and hands against his wheel-chair. Every poem seemed to me to contain jumbled insights into someone else. The lines were easy to pry apart. Their meaning was only lightly hidden behind the commonplace narrative of a collapsing love.

I left the café, and spent the rest of the afternoon pondering in Regent's Park. *Modern Love* is as incisive a description of the process of loss as I have ever read.

That night I met Gian Mario at a hotel bar in Soho.

'What did you find with your lady?'

'She is seventy-three. She still cycles and walks everywhere. She could do with a new pair of glasses. Her wrist hurts because she broke it, but it is not her diary-writing hand. She does not know how she lost the books. She did not even realise they were missing. She continues to write one to three thousand words a day.'

'Suicidal?'

'Not remotely.'

'Mad?'

I shook my head. 'Eccentric.'

'Happy?'

'Content,' I suggested. 'Not so discontented,' I corrected. 'Accepting,' I corrected again, and felt, as I said each word, that I chased Laura out of it. 'She says she is surprised. She hadn't expected to feel as well as she does since leaving the man Peter's house.'

Gian Mario bent forward until the top of his head almost reached the sugar bowl. When he straightened up he had a green book in his hand. Sextus Empiricus, *Outlines of Scepticism*. He gave the cover two stern taps, as though settling the contents inside. 'I must reheat the sceptical cabbage for you once again.'

Laura was not only in Meredith's poems, she was also in a two-thousand-year-old philosopher's account of 'how people struggle and eventually fail to discover the truth'.

'Sceptics become overwhelmed by the different and conflicting accounts of what happiness, justice, truth are all about. For every description, every argument, every theory, no matter how apparently compelling, another description, another argument, another theory exists that neutralises the former.'

'E attacking her one day, encouraging her the next?' I suggested excitedly. Gian Mario shook his head from side to side in a way that might have meant yes.

'One day the theory would be that E hated her; the next, that she loves her,' I continued, regardless. All it took, once again, was to translate the terms of the metaphor correctly. 'Another example: God has been wicked to Laura because he got her sacked from the public library. But God is good because he is providing her with the neuroses needed to be a true artist.'

'After a while, we find this condition of competing theories and arguments quite hard to take,' continued Gian Mario. 'It is exhausting, if not depressing. What next? Basically the Sceptic ends up saying, "Whatever." To me the sceptic elements of your lady's story amount to 1) her feeling of happiness as being completely unrelated to the actual achievements of her life, and to 2) the fact that such a feeling came unexpectedly. As soon as she gave up, as soon as she stopped waiting for one kind of happiness, some other form of happiness, or at least tranquillity, took over.'

I had to get back to Victoria station to catch the last train. It started to rain. The wind rattled shop doors and kicked boxes along the alleyways. As we walked down Oxford Street I remembered my voice recorder, and held it up to Gian Mario's face, but all I can hear now of what he calls his further 'lucubrations' is a scraping sound.

The last service to Eastbourne passes out of London in a sequence of diminishing sparkles. After the costume jewellery of Chelsea Bridge comes the glowing solder of Clapham Junction, then the embers of East Croydon. Twenty minutes later the train breaks through the North Downs into Sussex, where there is darkness.

Gian Mario was right – Laura was a practical example of scepticism, a two-thousand-year-old philosophy made flesh. Meredith was right – a messy love story combined with a desire to play a certain social role (the sensitive artist, in her case) was at the heart of Laura's unhappiness.

Everyone was right, except E.

'Here lies Laura Francis, who did nothing,' E began her proposed epitaph. Laura has done something for which she deserves to be remembered forever: she has written a forty-million-word description of being alive. If I were an extra-terrestrial wanting to understand humans, I wouldn't bother with literature or films or music, I'd go straight to Laura Francis. Life is never so distilled and simple as in a novel or a song. Laura deals with the daily murmur. Four decades before people began wearing portable computers twenty-four hours a day to record their physiological data and video their lives, Laura began a more perceptive work: a daily record of an ordinary woman's thoughts about her existence, written without any artfulness or false drama – written, so to speak, from the inside.

'Went nowhere', continues E.

Another lie. Laura did go somewhere. In 1974 she went to Rottingdean, in Sussex, with E.

'Was loved by nobody'.

This is more difficult. I want to be able to say that Laura was loved by lots of people – that E herself loved her, that Dame Harriette loved her, that Peter loved her. But I don't think they did. When she was young, her sisters and parents loved her, but that's not what E means. Apart from E, Laura never had a close friend.

Laura is funny, poignant, clever, perceptive, kind, generous, and has, against the probabilities, achieved something great in life with her diaries – but she remains Laura, an awkward woman at odds with the world. I am still learning what sort of person she is in real life, but in her books she is not a person who invites love, however much she might deserve it.

E's wrongness here isn't the fact of Laura's lack of love, it's how E places the blame. She suggests it is Laura's fault: too gauche, too bad-postured, too bursting with peculiarities to attract love. But the Laura she is talking about is a Laura she helped to create. That raw, exposed creature of the early diaries; the ill-tempered middle-aged cleaner at Peter's house – that was what was left of Laura once E had shorn her of love.

*

It was time to return the books. The skip had loaned them to Dido, and Dido had loaned them to me, and for five of the twelve years I had owned them I had been a gossipy god looking through solid walls into a person's privacy. And what had I seen? The muffled violence of an ordinary-extraordinary, mundanely outlandish, limp and taut life called Laura Francis.

And now Laura was discovered, and that part of my life was over. I had been privileged. Because I'm lucky enough not to have many principles and to like tittle-tattle, I'd opened the books and enjoyed myself for half a decade. There were no conclusions to draw. Scepticism, Meredithism, what instructive messages Laura's at first frightened and then entombed existence might hold for the rest of us; whether diaries do or do not accurately represent the people who write them – it was all so much nonsense and noise.

It was time to shut up.

A year after I met Laura for the first time, Dido died.

Her last days were ghastly. Just after a friendly nurse had inserted a drip into her arm at the local hospital, the odious consultant who'd been causing difficulties for some time insisted, through an intermediary, that the tubes be pulled out and Dido informed that there was, after all, no hope left. Horrified and defeated, she was transferred to the hospice. For three days the excellent staff there put her on what the government calls the Liverpool Pathway, which means drugging a person up until she can endure what is about to follow, then dehydrating her to death. Dido's flesh sank away as though it were being sucked into her bones.

I still wake up at 3 a.m. with nightmares about those days.

It wasn't until the morning of the funeral that I realised I had forgotten to invite Laura.

I raced up to the bungalow, but I was too late.

She was out. She had gone shopping with her sister in Newmarket.

# PART THREE
## *Biography*

# 31  Laura Penrose Francis

Feel pretty sure that I'll have something
published sometime in my life – either
artwork, or written work, or both;
it is inevitable, really, even if hard-won.

**Aged twenty-five**

**Laura Penrose Francis, May 22nd, 1939 –, *Diarist*.**
Father, Henry Francis (1913–1996), Mother, Dorothy Penrose
(1916–2012). Francis's early years were unsettled. Soon after
she was born, the family moved to St Just-in-Roseland,
Cornwall, where Francis's maternal grandfather, the Reverend
James Vavasor Hammond, was the Anglo-Catholic vicar of the
parish church. Her earliest memory is from the war: she
watched a solitary German plane fly over the village and drop
a bomb on a house flying the Union Jack. When the owner of
the house congratulated himself on his luck (because he had
happened to be out at the time of the attack), Francis's
grandfather reprimanded him: 'That was not luck, that was
providence.' The next day a cheque for £1,000 arrived at the
vicarage, signed by the house owner. The money enabled Rev
Hammond to put electricity in the church.

Francis's father was colour blind, so was not sent to the front
during the war. ('This probably saved his life.') An agricultural
engineer, he was given war work around Britain, including
training recruits for motorboats in Rothesay, Scotland. Francis's
mother, a classics graduate from Girton College, Cambridge,
moved with Laura to Cambridge. There they lived with

Laura's paternal grandparents at Whitefield House. It was not a happy time. Francis remembers her grandfather as a harsh and unloving man. On her father's return from war work, the family moved to Bedfordshire, where Francis and her younger sisters, Jennifer, Kate and Alison, grew up. Although she was a shy and generally isolated child, in her last year at primary school Francis's fellow students elected her to be May Queen, but the school authorities immediately decided she was not a suitable candidate and substituted the daughter of one of the dinner ladies instead. It was a first taste of the tenacious unfairness that Francis felt pursued her throughout her life. ('I agree with that!')

In 1951 Francis was given a diary for Christmas, and some green ink. ('That's why I began writing: I liked the green ink.')

This was the year after the family moved to Tudor House in Haynes Church End, near Bedford, a large sixteenth-century, and now Grade II listed building. 'The place was very isolated, not even a village – just a few houses, and a church. It was over a mile to the main road, where we caught the bus for school every day (eight miles). About half a mile away was a girls' boarding school called Hawnes, set in parkland. This was where my music teacher, Elsa Julich, was for a couple of years, until she had to leave, following a row with the headmistress. She then lodged with a kindly elderly couple who lived near our house. It was the time of the great smog in London. I remember the fog in Haynes, too.'

Francis was fourteen when she met the sixty-four-year-old Julich. Their love affair was never discussed between them explicitly, or consummated beyond a kiss; yet for twenty-six years this relationship with Julich dominated her life. The one exception was when Francis fell in love with a ninety-nine-year-old female nutritionist. Julich died in 1979.

Excited by men, impassioned by elderly women, Francis never married.

It is difficult for the reader of Francis's diaries not to be appalled by Julich's behaviour towards the young Francis, but in the early years of their relationship she was a kind friend who encouraged Francis's interest in writing and music. When Julich moved to Cambridge in 1953 to become an occasional music teacher for the Perse School for Girls, Francis followed in 1956. With the help of a family friend who sat on the board of governors, Francis persuaded her parents to send her to the school, and the school to have her. It was one of her few displays of academic effort ('I had to try twice. I was rejected the first time. But I was determined to get in'). During her time at the school, Francis again lived at Whitefield House. Now that her grandfather was dead, these were among the happiest years of her life. She took A-Levels in French (fail), French Literature (grade 2), English (grade 2) and Art ('a bad choice' – pass). She did not get into university.

In the early 1960s Francis pursued a series of disastrous part-time jobs as a librarian and a housekeeper-cook. For two years she was a student at the sixth-form Luton College of Technology, where she studied art. She must have appeared an odd figure. Five foot 10$^3$/$_4$, with a disdainful manner ('I think I was more shy'), agoraphobia and an inability to eat without choking, she was, at twenty, three years older than her teenage classmates.

From Luton, she won a place to study illustration at the fashionable Camberwell College of Art. London in 1962 was abuzz with innovative artists, musicians, writers; but it buzzed without Laura. After graduating, she worked briefly for an advertising agency and then, dogged by loneliness and lack of money, returned to Cambridge to work as a housekeeper. It was here that she met the leading nutritionist and micro-biologist Dr Harriette Chick DBE, and became her live-in companion for the three years before Dame Harriette's death in 1977, aged 102. Francis then continued in the same house and role, working for Chick's nephew, Peter Mitchell, for almost the next quarter of a century, until Professor Mitchell's death in 2001.

Laura Francis's distinction as the most prolific known diarist in history (according to *The Guinness Book of Records*, the previous record-holder is a 'newspaperman', Edward Robb Ellis, twenty-two million words) would have gone undiscovered but for the fact that 148 volumes of the diaries were thrown into a skip by builders after she was evicted following Professor Mitchell's death. By good luck a Cambridge academic, Professor Richard Grove, was playing in the building site and spotted the books. He donated them to Dr Dido Davies, who five years later handed the collection over to the biographer Alexander Masters.

It took Masters five years to discover Francis's identity.

Today, happier, though not happy, Francis continues to write several thousand words a day, much of it still about what she has seen on television. She does not know how the books Professor Grove discovered ended up in the skip; she suggests they were discarded during the solicitors' hasty efforts to evict her from Professor Mitchell's house following his death. She had not missed them; she never looks at old diary entries. The moment she closes the back cover on a completed volume, she loses interest in it.

Since she left Professor Mitchell's house, the purpose of her journal has changed again. Now, she says, she no longer writes to relieve frustration, hide love, provide protection or to exhaust her teeming mind.

She keeps going now simply because 'I like the sound of the

pen on the page.' Her style is immediate and unself-conscious. It rarely takes her more than six weeks to fill an entire notebook, often writing between two and three thousand words a day.

When Masters turned up at the door of Francis's bungalow in 2012, sixty years after she began her diary in 1952, she was unsurprised.

'She spoke,' he said, 'as if she had been expecting me all along.'

# 32  PS

I have seen Laura many more times since our first meeting.
We have become friends. Two weeks ago I gave her the full
manuscript of this book to read.

It must be a rule of writing biographies about unknown
people that the subject agrees to everything you have put down.
It is otherwise too easy to get some small fact wrong, or to insist
on a false interpretation that might seem minor to you but could,
for reasons you hadn't appreciated, ruin your subject's life. With
famous people it doesn't matter so much – they have lots of ways
to defend themselves. But as a biographer of unknown people
you must be exceptionally careful not to trash someone who has
no capacity to reply. If you cannot reach a version of the book
that both you and your subject are prepared to accept, then the
whole thing must go on the fire.

Laura has objected to two things.

I have changed neither of them.

Both are pictures. The most prolific diarist in history is not
fussed about the words.

Her first objection concerns the photograph on page 168, of a
woman standing on a pedestal holding a bow and arrow.

Laura:  I don't like it that she has no clothes on.
Me:     But she does have clothes on – it's a white body suit to
        make her look like a marble statue. Do you object to
        marble statues?
Laura:  My love for E was never like *that*.

The second is the photograph on page 170, of E on a bicycle, aged seventy-two. It is not a picture of E. Laura has never seen this woman before. It seems that there were two unknown bodies in the skip that day in 2001 when Richard and Dido pushed through a hedge to trespass about a building site.

Apart from that, Laura has approved the manuscript. She does not mind the fact that I suspected her of being mad; she is not worried about my exposure of her crushes on E or Dame Harriette; she is happy for me to go on and on and on about her failures as an artist.

It is all, she says, 'jolly swerbles'.

# Acknowledgements

This book could not have been finished without Flora Dennis (pictured here dancing, thank goodness, with me). Her superb editorial suggestions; her cunning ideas about structure and plot; her impatience with my tendency to pontificate; her ability to read (and with each reading, improve) the same pages over and over and over and over again until they are fit to be published or there is no hope left and they must be thrown out – her decisive influence on the writing of this book has been invaluable.

It astonishes me that Dido Davies is dead. I cannot believe that her name and death go together. She provided the diaries; she gave this book its direction; she worked brilliantly on the early chapters; and she taught me how to write it all, starting thirty years ago when she, a newly-elected English Fellow, crawled through the window of my college bar and said hello. This is her last self-portrait, drawn in her hospital bed:

She is buried in Coton churchyard, just outside Cambridge.

Richard Grove is another shock. Before his accident Richard was the leading academic in the field of environmental history, a subject he helped to found. His enviable (and sometimes maddening) wayward character led him to break into a building site where he had no business to be, and discover the diaries. It is because of people such as Richard that the best things happen.

Laura Francis: for a moment she held four years of my life in the balance. As I sat in her bungalow, explaining that I had read her private diaries and wanted to publish her biography, she would have been quite within her rights to kick me out of the door. I expected her to. But without hesitation she agreed to let me continue work, and has been nothing but delightful ever since.

There have been a great many people who have helped me with this book, either directly, or indirectly by their support and friendship. Barbara Weaver (graphologist), Patricia Field (graphologist) and Vince Johnson (detective), three of the experts I consulted, are different characters but shared one essential quality: an immediate understanding of the importance and interest of Laura's forgotten life. Richard Goldthwaite, Gian Mario Cao, Iain Fenlon: the richness of their humour and their curiosity about Laura were central to the final third of the story. Graeme Mitchison has been vital in two areas, as a pianist and as a scientist. He explained and demonstrated the importance of the *Pathétique*, and checked (and corrected) my forays into physics metaphors. I could not have done without this insightful and cultured man. Here is a picture of me chasing after him on a bicycle:

I want also to thank Vinita Damodaran, Richard's wife, for her permission to include Richard and the story of his car accident, and her heroic support of Richard; Caroline and Nick Dennis, who were among the first to read the diaries: their interest in them, and encouraging comments, inspired me to push on; Joan Brady made, as always, clever and helpful suggestions about how I should write the story; John Rogers, my ex-school teacher and first publisher, for his memorable thoughts about the Trinity.

James Blishen, Adrian Clarke and Brendan Griggs, Fanny Johnson, Miraphora Mina, for reading and checking the ms; Ruth Ur, for her comments, and also her enthusiasm for the idea and her lovely house in France, where she makes me repaint the window ledges; Sarah Burbidge, Nathan Graves and Lucy Graves, for editorial suggestions, gin cocktails and being blissful gougers. Belinda, Diana and Curtis Allan, for the use of their house in Italy – it is the best place to write. Andrew and Otto Barrow, Charles Collier, James Cormick, Jonathan Foyle, Andy Grove, Hugh Hardinge, Cathy Hembry, Diane Johnson, Michael Lee, Kate Lewis, Annie Maccoby, Cornelius Medvei, Colin Midson, Natalie Shaw, Julia Walsh – all of these have given good advice, cheered me up when I'm low and made the four years it took me to write this book, and the fifteen years it took me to think about it, a pleasure.

To whom this may concern at the Department of Culture, Media and Sport: whatever the funding for public libraries is at the moment, please double it. The Cambridgeshire Collection at the Cambridge Public Library has been an essential resource. My thanks also to the Perse School for Girls, in particular to vice-principal Dr Helen Stringer and to Catherine Hanlon, the excellent (but now former) librarian.

At Fourth Estate, I have been supported by four first-class people in particular, who have been there from the time I first joined this publisher: Nicholas Pearson, Michelle Kane, Julian Humphries and Robert Lacey (sitting in the office, his pen is scratching out the last dangling particles from the proofs even as I write this). Every three or four years I pop up babbling about something or other; they always receive me with generosity and coffee. I also thank Vera Brice, for her help in designing these picture-strewn pages, and Anna Morrison, for her design of the cover. Peter Straus, my splendid literary agent with a scary habit of going suddenly silent on the phone – he has been the perfect guide and companion.

Fran Reynolds and Christy Grimes, the two eagle-eyed readers who spotted a critical error in the first edition (I'd stupidly given away Not-Mary's real name, dozens of pages too early): thank you – that's been corrected in this printing.

Denise Knoweldon typed up many passages from the diaries, including several entire volumes, encouraged me to press on and helped me to understand the best way to keep track of the themes and characters in Laura's notebooks; Dominic Nutt had nothing to do with this book, but a lot to do with the other work I did during the time of writing it, and so that was good; Elisa Vedova, Alison Tyler and Helena Geer, for their help in looking after baby Ida and the house. To Sabrina and Charles Harcourt-Smith, my thanks for being sympathetic landlords. To Amanda Harcourt and AJ, Leslie and Dave, my thanks for being good neighbours. Nothing is worse for the concentrated study of five million words, cramped into 148 volumes of diaries, than the wrong people next door.

Finally, to Ida:

who is two and cannot read.